P9-AOT-548

FAITH AND LEARNING

FAITH AND LEARNING

CHRISTIAN FAITH AND HIGHER EDUCATION IN TWENTIETH CENTURY AMERICA

ALEXANDER MILLER

To think well is to serve God in the interior court.

THOMAS TRAHERNE

GREENWOOD PRESS, PUBLISHERS
WESTPORT, CONNECTICUT

Library of Congress Cataloging in Publication Data

Miller, Alexander, 1908-1960.
Faith and learning.

Reprint of the 1960 ed. published by Association Press, New York.
Bibliography: p.
1. Church and college in the United States.
I. Title.
[LC383.M5 1977] 377'.8'0973 77-23142
ISBN 0-8371-9458-X

Originally published in 1960 by Association Press, New York

Reprinted with the permission of Association Press

Reprinted in 1977 by Greenwood Press, Inc.

Library of Congress catalog card number 77-23142

ISBN 0-8371-9458-X

Printed in the United States of America

For

DAVID

whose generation will know
more about these matters.

CONTENTS

FOREWORD

This book is published during the period when the National Student Christian Federation and its member movements are engaged in a major project on *The Life and Mission of the Church.* This project, initiated by the World's Student Christian Federation, is an attempt on the part of students in many countries to rethink their responsibility as Christians in the world. In the United States it was decided to place major emphasis during the academic year 1960-1961 on The Church's Mission in the Colleges and Universities. The discussion will be guided and stimulated by contributions from many sides. This book by Alexander Miller is therefore welcome at this time. He builds on the debate of "The University Question" to which men like Arnold Nash, John Coleman, and Walter Moberly have contributed so brilliantly. The book provides a context in which the main issues facing Christians in the academic world can be fruitfully discussed. Whether or not its point of view is accepted, it will raise significant questions and should prove helpful to student groups, faculty, and administrators in clarifying their own views.

The book has its origin in a proposal to Professor Miller by the Study Committee of the United Student

Christian Council (now incorporated into the National Student Christian Federation) that he set down his thinking with regard to the main problems affecting the church and the university. We are grateful to Professor Miller for his willingness to take up this request.

THOMAS WIESER
National Student Christian Federation

PREFACE

To write on the relation of Faith and Learning is a "holy ground" undertaking, not only because of the high solemnity of the issues themselves, but because the ground has been sanctified by the devoted labor of the best of men, from Clement of Alexandria to John Calvin of Geneva, from Augustine to Newman and into our own time. Not only so, but Christian thought in this area has been stimulated by those who loved learning and the Community of Learning, while withholding allegiance to Christian faith and to the Christian church, or even resenting and resisting the claims of Faith and Church as inimical to the things they cared for. "Which of the prophets," they have sometimes had to say to the church, "have not your fathers stoned?"

So the Christian writer on the things of the mind comes chastened to the work, for we Christians have made mistakes here, some of them "beauts" (as Fiorello La Guardia used to say of his rare blunders). Our patchy record ought to keep us passably humble, even if the issues themselves were not so awesome.

But the issues *are* awesome, and of quite peculiar difficulty.

> What has Athens to do with Jerusalem, the Academy with the church? What is there in common between the philosopher and the Christian, between the pupil of Hellas and the pupil of Heaven?

The Western world found a wiser way than the rejection of the world's wisdom implied in Tertullian's question here, but the question remains. Though the church refused to keep faith celibate from culture, and at times hoped for a happy marriage, the marriage relation in fact has never been easy: frequent tiffs and not infrequent quarrels, and latterly something like an agreed separation that might issue in divorce if either could be happy without the other. But just recently there are renewed signs that church and culture can no more live without each other than they could live with each other, and we may have the makings of a reconciliation. There is more to be said about that in Chapter One.

Certainly there has been much talk of reconciliation, and some premature announcements of it. This book suggests conditions that might make it hopeful, but refuses to promise anything. Both partners to the problem are too spritely to go easily into double harness. At least we know what caused the trouble before, and what makes for difficulty now. And we know this because over the last years a number of those who deplore the separation have labored to overcome it, most fruitfully when they loved both church and culture and were personally torn in their separation.

When I was first commissioned to write this book,

I began to accumulate what I assumed to be the necessary raw materials for a responsible attack on the problem. I designated a desk for the project, and began to stack on it the piled-up wisdom on which I hoped to draw. But before long the desk itself was hidden, and I myself buried like a mole beneath a mound of material positively frightening in its bulk. Not only did I have several linear feet of "indispensable" books, but the accumulated files of *Religious Education, The Christian Scholar,* and other journals devoutly concerned with these issues. Add bulging file-folders, and the whole situation was intimidating, since I was supposed to distill from these "makings" a modest and, hopefully, a readable book. I swear I went through most of it, and most of it was valuable: but it was vastly repetitive, and eventually I had to risk identifying that "iron ration" of source material which I think represents our best resource for dealing with the problem of Faith and Learning over the next period.

The present book was commissioned partly in response to a vague feeling, issuing sometimes in loose talk, that we needed "an American Moberly." The reference is to Sir Walter Moberly's *The Crisis in the University,* which was written in Britain in 1949 and republished over here.[1] It has been an invaluable resource for those who grapple with the problems of

[1] Moberly explains that his book is the fruit of discussion among Christian university teachers, which had issued earlier in a series of *University Pamphlets,* published by the Student Christian Movement Press. That earlier series is still worth attention.

Faith and Learning, and for those too who are concerned simply with the role of the university and the integrity of its life. It would be silly and pretentious to claim that what follows fills the bill; but it is written somewhat with Moberly in mind, for his book is the most influential in a list of books which represent a profound Christian concern with higher education. It became articulate, as far as this generation was concerned, with Arnold Nash's *The University in the Modern World,* which was followed by Moberly's book and by John Coleman's *The Task of the Christian in the University.*[2] In my own judgment these are among the most important contributions to a discussion which grows more urgent and more promising by the day.

The immediate justification for the present book is that none of these items serves our contemporary case; Nash and Coleman's books for the sufficient reason that they are out of print; Moberly's because, though its essential argument is indispensable and we shall draw on it freely, it is too British in its reference to do full justice to the particular problems of the American situation.

In any event, as the situation develops, more and younger people are involved in the discussion, among them many who know not Moberly. Part of what follows, therefore, is an unashamed paraphrase of material which will be familiar enough to those who have worked over the ground during the last decade. It

[2] For documentation of these books, see Bibliography.

needs to be restated, though, before we can move on. I have drawn liberally, also, on two books which originate outside this short "tradition," but which are of immense importance. The first is John Henry Newman's *The Scope and Nature of University Education,*[3] surely the wisest and most eloquent of all the books ever written about the university, by one who cherished faith and who loved learning, and was not prepared to have either despoiled, even by the other. The second is George H. Williams' *The Theological Idea of the University,* which gathers up the meaning of a long tradition that is rich in insight concerning the dialectic between faith and knowledge, and the conditions under which each may rebuke, refresh, and reinforce the other.[4]

Without all these what follows could have small chance of being of use in our present dilemmas. It levies on them freely, not always with express acknowledgment, and goes on to project lines of advance based on personal reflection, considerable group discussion, and some practical pedagogical experience. But if the writer reaches any height of authentic vision at all, it is because he stands on others' shoulders. In any event

[3] This is an accessible edition of the bulk of the material which was earlier printed as *The Idea of a University.* The full version of *The Idea . . .* has been reissued while this book was in process, but *The Scope and Nature . . .* has the gist of the matter, and more than enough material for our purpose.

[4] The short Bibliography at the end of the book gives publishers' data on these central items, and lists also a very select few of the books which fill out various aspects of the matter, and will serve as introduction to a fuller study of it.

its worth and usefulness are limited partly by considerations of space, and partly by the preoccupations of the writer: for example, it takes scant account of the particular practical and constitutional problems of state and municipal colleges. Since one must concentrate somewhere, the concentration in this case is theological rather than practical or constitutional; but the discussion goes on.

Part of the material has been used in connection with the Verhulst Lectureship at the University of Wisconsin, and in more informal ways elsewhere. It has had the benefit of much discussion, and of comment by colleagues both at Stanford and in New York. In this process defects both of form and of content have been eliminated: where they remain, it is because I have been stubborn even when my friends have been candid.

The book was first proposed by the Study Committee of the United Student Christian Council, which is now incorporated within the National Student Christian Federation. It is planned to be of use in the ongoing discussions of the Federation and its affiliated movements: but it is hoped that it may also win the attention of two other groups: (1) Christian men and women who share responsibility for the work of learning: teachers, trustees, administrators, students, campus workers, ministers related to colleges; and (2) those inquiring intellectuals whose concern for the work of education is such that they will gladly pick up clues where they can, even from the Christians!

CHAPTER ONE

SIGNS OF THE INTELLECTUAL TIMES

Around thirty years ago, when the present writer was an undergraduate in New Zealand, those of us who were trying to live by a Christian commitment were eager to carry that commitment into various areas of the common life: we were active to strike a blow for economic justice and to organize the world for peace. The one area that never came under our Christian scrutiny, to the best of my rusty recollection, was the scholarly work we were committed to do and the scholarly institution in which we did it. The Christian Faith and Economic Justice . . . The Christian Faith and the Cause of Peace . . . these were our daily business and our intellectual stock in trade. But never do I recall so much as a single lecture, formal discussion, or bull session on the relation of Christian Faith and Higher Education, or about the Christian use of the tools of the scholar's trade. In point of fact, the effect of our social preoccupations was to trim to the minimum the time and effort we could give to scholarly work; and I have a notion that even if we did not think of the demands of the curriculum as a nuisance which interfered with more vital human and Christian concerns, we were at least prepared without twinge of conscience to consider scholarly accomplishment a prize well lost for more important causes.

From what I know of the situation the same was true of the United States.

It is with the United States that we are presently concerned, and here observers are of one mind: that over the last generation the changes are spectacular, so that now we have a church profoundly concerned about the work of the mind and the institutions in which it is done, and a university increasingly hospitable to the penetration of "religion," increasingly accessible to Christian comment on the meaning of the scholarly task. An older intransigence to the penetration of piety is giving way to a readiness at least for conversation, and a kind of generalized and often inchoate willingness on the part of the colleges to "do something about religion."

Causes of Awakened Interest in "Religion"

The causes of the change are hard to identify. Some of them are immediate and visible; others derive from the longer history of church and university, which belonged together in their origins, and are no more at ease with their "bill of divorcement" than they had been when they were "married." In order to understand both the opportunities and the dangers of the present situation we must make a try at explaining how it has come about.

The immediate causes are probably the least important. There are certain vaguely pious pressures to do away with the exclusion of religion from higher education. They come from parents who not only are concerned that their young people avoid divorce and delinquency, but who recognize that they themselves have lacked that frame of loyalty which would have given their lives a shape and their children a heritage of religious and moral commitment. They come from alumni and the general public, vaguely anxious because they conceive that the American way of life, as they understand it, is threatened by subversion from within and by aggression from without, and feel that in some ill-understood fashion the stability of the established order depends on a religious resource now sadly corroded. Most important of all, in this area of immediate pressure, is a pervasive and growing discontent among students themselves. They are restless with their own illiteracy in matters of faith; they know that their intellectual grasp of their formal religious heritage is disreputable and poor. They are not content that as their intellectual life matures, their religion should stay adolescent. And they know even better than their parents can tell them that the shapeless life is no more worth living than the unexamined one.

These factors together with others mean simply that the contemporary and much-debated "revival of religion" spills over onto the campus, whose walls are not high enough to keep back the tide, even if the will were any longer there.

The so-called "religious revival," in some of its manifestations so patently superficial, is yet potentially influential and it requires some explanation. None of the obvious possibilities fully accounts for it. Probably when ministers are asked about the notable increase in numbers of people in their churches they would point first of all to the concern of young families about the nurture of their children; but though this is a real problem it is not a new one, and it did not formerly breed the volume of church affiliation we have had during the years since World War II. The crisis of the times and the pressure of anxiety sounds plausible as an explanation; but there have been other times and places where crises were more extreme and the pressures more immediate—I think, for example, of London under the bombing during the war itself—yet these situations did not always or even regularly produce a boom in piety such as we now experience.

Actually, like any other pervasive and influential movement in American life, its roots go deep into the history of the nation and the long rhythm of its life. It is neither necessary nor possible to tell the whole story; but there are certain elements in the history which do something to explain the present movement, and which are relevant also to the development of the university, and to developments in the university affecting the prospects for religion.

The shape of American religious life is probably determined in the main by two periods in the history: the first, *the "classical" or Colonial period*; and the second, *the period of the migrations* especially between the end of the Civil War and the end of the nineteenth century.[1]

1. *The dominance of New England in the formative years* determined that American life would be laid down on a Puritan Protestant base. And the cultural effect of this was momentous. It may be illustrated from three areas:

a. Christianity was carried to these United States by a Puritan class of small proprietors and their professional affiliates—doctors, teachers, lawyers, clergy. It was this group which became the *business* class in American society (what the sociologists call "the old middle class"). Summarily the effect of this was twofold: in the first place, it gave to the dominant forms of American Christianity a cast determined by the business mind and the business interest; but, in the second place, and this positively, it gave to the American business community a degree of responsibility which is not unrelated to its unexpected capacity for self-criticism and internal reformation.

b. The *political* patterns of American life are inexplicable apart from Calvinist elements derived from New England. It was Calvinist realism about man, joined to the practical political wisdom drawn from the long experience of the West, which made the form of American democracy and determined that even Jeffer-

[1] The most recent and relevant account we have of the history and sociology of the American religious communities is in Will Herberg's *Protestant-Catholic-Jew* (New York: Doubleday & Co., Inc., 1955).

son would act with a political astuteness hardly to be explained by his own unchastened optimism about man. "Good government," as he said in a somewhat un-Jeffersonian accent, "is founded in jealousy and not in confidence."

c. It was Puritan New England which put the stamp of its influence upon the first and most influential centers of higher learning in America. We shall be back to this again; but for the moment it is enough to say that *it was Puritan Protestantism which gave to the New England colleges and, by the same token, to American higher education the last coherent account of its own function*; which was in effect to supply not only "a learned clergy" (though that formulation regularly appears), but a learned leadership to both church and state, a professional class equipped by liberal learning for an understanding of its full and proper role, and of course a succession generation by generation to the Guild of Scholars itself, on whose quality and character the other functions depended.[2]

2. The original Puritan deposit has been overlaid by *the development of religious pluralism,* which dates substantially from the mass migrations of the nineteenth century, most significantly from the period after the Civil War. Herberg has done a definitive account of

[2] The relation of New England Puritanism to the contributions of Virginia, Maryland, and Pennsylvania—both in politics and in education—will perhaps be always in dispute. This is not the place to argue it, though I should think that my very restrained generalizations could be defended.

these movements in *Protestant-Catholic-Jew*, and has demonstrated, I think beyond question, that the bulk and form of contemporary piety depend on the history and sociology of the religious communities, measured roughly over three generations from the fourth quarter of last century.

The first-generation immigrants moved into America bearing with them their own ethnic religion. It was *nominally* Catholic, or Protestant, or Jewish, but it was *substantially* Polish or Irish or Italian Catholic, Polish or German Jewish, Danish or German Protestant. The aspiration of this first generation was to keep the ethnic heritage alive, and the ethnic differential was potent enough even to condition the character of the religious community, determining its choice of priests and the language of its services, barring even intermarriage within the same religious community which would have blurred the ethnic lines. The first generation, that is to say, was pious after the fashion of the fathers. Its religion was, in one powerful aspect, a means to ethnic cohesion; and those elements in the religion were resisted which would have qualified the solidity of the ethnic group.

But there were laid down, in the matrix of American life, forces too strong for the ethnic bond: forces cultural and industrial which created an interdependence transcending ethnic lines. The second generation felt the strength of the American way and the lure of the American dream, and was eager to escape the ghetto and launch out into the full current of American life.

Its aspiration was not isolation but assimilation; and to achieve this the second generation shed the ethnic markings, the language, the diet, the religion of the fathers. There was a double inducement to shed the religion, because during the first years of this century strong tides of secularism were sweeping across the American cultural scene, so that to be Americanized was to be secularized, to abandon what were thought of as the superstitions of the fathers for the strong confidence in reason of which Dewey was the symbol, and the astringent cynicism which made H. L. Mencken the darling of the secular gods.

But "what the son wishes to forget, the grandson wishes to remember": the third generation finds that to be part of the American "everybody" is to be in effect a "nobody," and begins to search for some principle of self-identification. There develops a nostalgia for the ethnic heritage, reinforced no doubt by a growing sense of the thinness of the secular option. Certain elements of the heritage cannot be recovered. It would be wasteful to relearn the language, but there is a certain toying with traditional dishes as a minimum relief from the all-pervasive American hamburger.

Most significant is the realization that the one element of the heritage that matters most can in fact be most readily recovered, and that without qualifying one's Americanism—namely, the faith of the fathers. That can be recovered, but not quite in the old form of it: for over the last two generations the long and strong traditions of the three great religious communities have been, on the whole, *too* strong for the ethnic varieties of them. So instead of a multiplicity of ethnic churches there are now three salient options—Protestant, Catholic, Jew. By the sociological logic of these three generations America has become pious again, and pious after a triadic fashion. And so pervasive is this triadic religious expression that it becomes on the one hand desperately *superficial* (Herberg demonstrates how easily this pervasive piety goes together with a thorough secularism in day-to-day practice); and yet so coincidental with "Americanism" that it becomes *oppressive and persecuting,* so that to be divorced from all three of the "official" religious communities—to be a frank and outspoken atheist, for example, and how rare they are!—is to be suspect of un-American tendencies.[3]

It is not suggested by Herberg or by anyone else that history and sociology wholly account for such movements of the human spirit as may be represented in the "religious revival"; but since we mentioned the prevalent piety as one of the factors which created a new hospitality to "religion" on the campuses of the nation, it seemed necessary to notice that its roots go

[3] One of our leading reviews published, within the last year or two, an article by an honest atheist mother who had tried, as a good mother should, to bring her children up in the unbelief which was her own working "faith," only to find that when at school they denied that they were "anything"—that is, denied that they were either Protestant, Catholic, or Jew—they were suspected by the other children of being at best odd, at worst subversive. Her article was titled: "Won't Somebody Tolerate Me?"

far back into the heritage. The contemporary effect of it, in terms of our present problem, is twofold:

> In the first place, it generates the inchoate demand that institutions of higher learning "do more about religion" than they have done over the last generation, and by the same token threatens the colleges and universities with a piety of quite incredible superficiality.
>
> In the second place, the triadic character of American "religion" means that it becomes impossible to discuss the relation of the Community of Faith to the Community of Culture, as in the course of the argument we shall be bound to do, without taking serious acount of the fact that in contemporary America—as distinct, for example, from mediaeval Europe—the Community of Faith is a triadic community.

Both of these, as we shall see, have crucial and concrete implications for our discussion. But the possibility of a new and fruitful encounter between Faith and Learning, and between the Community of Faith and the Community of Learning, rests on factors deeper and more fundamental than these. It depends not upon the pervasiveness of piety, nor on vague pious pressures upon the university, but upon the fact that both the Community of Faith and the Community of Learning are coming to a new self-consciousness. Partly in response, no doubt, to the stress of the times, both church and university are driven to assess their own resources, and to seek such further resources out of their traditions as help them to be true to their authentic nature and to perform rightly their contemporary work. And the more seriously they take their separate commissions, the more they are drawn to discuss their relation each with the other, and to engage again in the age-old dialectic between faith and knowledge, or between the knowledge that is the fruit of love and the knowledge that is the work of reason.

The Theological Revival

Even if the tide of popular religion recedes, as it shows some signs of doing, important ground has been gained that need not be lost again. Most important for our purpose is the fact that within the amorphous religiosity of our time is a core of religious substance, a theological renaissance of tremendous potency and vitality. It is confined to no one denomination and to no one continent, but infects the whole of Christendom. My own judgment is that the most vital phase of it is in these United States, possibly for the reason that whatever weaknesses American Christianity may have shown from time to time, it has never lost a concern for the problems of the common life. The "Social Gospel" of a generation ago was theologically superficial, but at least it represented a Christian concern for culture; so that what has happened over the last generation is that the spokesmen for American Protestantism have taken a biblical theology which in its European form tends to aridity and detachment, and wedded it to a cultural concern to make a synthesis best represented by Reinhold Niebuhr, though not alone by him. The effect of this is to give us a recovery of classical and biblical Christianity vital enough to enliven and unite the church, to open communication of a lively sort between Protestant and Catholic, and between a Christianity newly aware of its Hebraic roots and a Jewry ever more conscious of its heritage. And all this in close relation to a secular culture probing at the depths of its personal and social experience, and beginning persistently to ask the existential questions to which biblical faith also addresses itself, whether its specific answers be accepted or refused.

If I had been a university administrator or teacher a generation ago I should have been wary of any approaches by a religious community which was so sorely divided, was clearly fumbling after an adequate expression of its own faith, and in certain of its manifestations was so hostile to free inquiry and to the life of the mind—especially of the scientific mind. Many of those who think for the university are still infected with revulsion from a piety which in their own earlier experience was the enemy of intellectual integrity, and from which they accordingly broke free. But the situation now is that the university confronts a church which is confident, relatively unified, chastened by its own cultural failures, and consequently far less strident in its reaction to intellectual inquiry—obviously capable of articulating, out of a venerable heritage, a relevant contemporary word.

The University Question

The Community of Learning, for its part, is also a good deal chastened by the experience of the last generation. Having entered into its full freedom, it finds itself bereft of any principle of order. It is not only that extreme specialization threatens the cohesion of the university as a community of scholars, but it finds itself straightly charged with failing to provide those under its tutelage with the ingredients of valid decision, far less a coherent "philosophy of life." And even if the university is inclined to reject full responsibility at this point, it still has to settle in some normative fashion how much or how little responsibility for the making of men it will in fact accept.

The problem goes even deeper; for it is one thing to stand for the dignity of the life of the mind, as it is the instinct of the university to do, but it is another thing to validate it. It is peculiarly difficult to defend it when it becomes patent that mere sophistication, especially of the scientific sort, is a two-edged weapon which is potent both for mischief and for health.

It is not only the interior life of the university which has to be grounded in a new rationale: it is necessary also to find some principle of order as between the university and the demands of the wider society. On the one hand, the gains of the scientific method are often put to dubious use; on the other hand, the demands of the wider society for military and technological equipment tend to press out of shape the traditional form of the university, which was meant to represent a balanced concern for a total cultural heritage, without regard at all to its "utility." But what *gave* the heritage its sanctity, and what principle of order is to hold the university in balance?

All these questions are for fuller discussion as the argument moves along. I have been concerned only to suggest here that the new hospitality of the university to the witness of the church is not the result only of particular pious pressures, which may be mischievous as well as helpful. It stems, on the one hand, from the fact that the church has come through to a new articulateness and relevance and, on the other, from the fact that the university faces dilemmas difficult to be resolved out of its own present resources. This does not at all mean that the university is in any mood to put itself under theological tutelage again; but it does mean that it is less self-confident and more ready to pick up clues where it can. The effect is that the university's interior debate about its own nature and function can readily be widened to take in the contribution of the theologian, provided the latter can demonstrate that he brings to the discussion a concern for the university's own integrity and effectiveness, and that he has no personal or professional axe to grind. Here as elsewhere the condition of effective criticism is disinterested devotion: and the value of the materials on which we shall chiefly draw is that they are generated out of profound love for the Commonwealth of Learning, and a concern to be good citizens within it.

Though our particular business will be with the relation of religion and higher education, we ought, as we go about it, to learn a good deal about the Christian faith itself, about the grounds on which it rests and the ways in which it can be communicated, and about the service which Christian men owe to the communities of their loyalty.

CHAPTER TWO

THE UNIVERSITY AS A PROBLEM TO ITSELF

We shall be reviewing some of the very trenchant criticism which has been leveled, in some part by Christian commentators, at the contemporary university. In the measure that it has relevance, and some potential usefulness, it is grounded in a high sense of the dignity of the scholarly enterprise and the richness of the university tradition. One of the most moving and exhilarating things about life in the university community, even in these days when it is sorely troubled, is the sense that one's own concern for the integrity of the university, nourished out of Christian faith, is deeply shared by many men who confess no Christian commitment at all, but who are exemplars of good citizenship in the Republic of Letters, and by the same token good comrades in the struggle for its freedom and its well-being.

The University's Calling

What is it that gives to so many men, otherwise divided from one another by basic commitment, the sense that as members of the university they are fellow citizens of no mean city, that the community of scholars is a fatherland whose life is to be cherished and whose frontiers are to be defended? Surely it is that the university, through all distractions and betrayals, has on it the marks of its origins, has in trust a very rich inheritance, and is committed to a calling upon whose faithful performance the authentic well-being of the human community depends.

This vivid sense of participation and of dedication is nourished, I think, by three factors.

In the first place, there is the sense that the custody and transmission of the cultural heritage is an enterprise of high importance and great exhilaration. It embodies both the sense of achievement and the sense of adventure—"the pride of intellectual penetration and the awe before the impenetrable mystery." Out of this tradition can best be distilled an understanding of what makes us men, and of what makes us the kind of men we are. Here are to be found the roots both of our conviction and of our prejudice, the best confirmation of the former and the best corrective of the latter. In serious dealing with the heritage we discover that the questions which are jolted out of us by the impact of personal and present reality have been asked before and variously answered, yet never in so definitive a way that we are relieved of the right and the responsibility to try the answers "on our own pulses." The tradition is spacious enough to make us breathe a wider air than fills the narrow room of our own intellect, and it has in it enough variety of interest and emphasis to chasten dogmatism, check stridency of thought and word, and teach a certain delicacy in the discussion and dissection of the issues of life. As Newman puts it, "Certainly a liberal education does manifest itself in a courtesy, propriety and polish of word and action, which is beautiful in itself and acceptable to others; but it does much more. It brings the mind into shape. . . ."[1] Newman's old-world language is not ours; but we too have to learn that precision and delicacy in the handling of the heritage which is born of the knowledge that here is a wealth of wisdom which is precious in itself and necessary for our self-understanding. We win the right to improve it only by devoutly appropriating it.

It is the university's intimate preoccupation with the human heritage that gives to membership in it that zest and devotion which generates the best of its work. Of course there is a jaded and degenerate variety of teaching and learning which is no better than "the bland leading the bland," but there is no hope in it and small satisfaction—it need only be borne, it need not be approved. And even here there is always the possibility—the Christian would say by the grace of Heaven—that existential truth may take the decadent scholar by the scruff of his withered neck.

In the second place, to be accepted into membership in the university is to enter into a succession of the men of the mind, for the university has its own scroll of heroes, its own chronicle of conflict, and its own hard-won victories. There is no need to romanticize it,

[1] See Bibliography for source of all excerpts from John Henry Newman.

for it was made by men, men subject to bigotry and blindness, as all men are. But they wrought well enough to give us more than we deserve and more than we can live up to without the aid of their example.

The history of the university has been so often told that it need here be only summarized.[2] There were forerunners of it in India as early as the sixth century before Christ, in "monasteries" and ashrams where teachers shared with eager inquirers a wisdom which even then was ancient. In the Near East, even before Islam, there were schools strong enough to attract exiles from the Greek academies, and this stream of learning was caught up into the tide of Islamic scholarship that also gathered into itself the learning of Greece, which had culminated in the work of Plato and Aristotle. Christian Rome before the fall of the Empire had sought a consolidation of Greek learning and the revealed truth of the Gospel, and some part of that structure survived across the dark centuries to be joined again with Arabic scholarship within the ordered world of the Middle Ages. Even before the flowering of the twelfth century there are signs of a loose-knit international community of scholars who with Christian diligence attempted not only to apply the truth of revelation but to conserve the work of reason. But it was the founding of the University of Paris in the end of the twelfth century that marks the begin-

[2] For what follows we are much indebted to John Coleman, *The Task of the Christian in the University*, which is unhappily no longer available.

ning of the continuing tradition which has put its mark on all our modern schools. Its substantial freedom from local ecclesiastical and civil authority was secured to it by papal edict (we shall return to this in Chapter Three); and with Bologna and Salerno, Oxford and Cambridge, the foundation of the university tradition was well and truly laid. In their heyday these were not so much separate universities as "component parts of one integral university," so that students and teachers moved freely from one center to another within a cosmopolitan community of learning. The rise of nationalism sundered the universities from one another, but it rapidly increased their number: so that it was from the English foundations that the bridge was built to the New World, with the establishment of Harvard College.

But the very word *university* (*universitas*), though it now has only the distant sense of that "all of you together" which referred originally to the cosmopolitan community of scholars, still represents an aspiration after the situation in which the pooled wisdom of many men can generate a wisdom more sage and more balanced than the summed knowledge of them all. It was this that Newman was after when he spoke of his own hope that the university might be a place where "An assemblage of learned men, zealous for their own sciences, and rivals of each other, are brought, by familiar intercourse and for the sake of intellectual peace, to adjust together the claims and relations of their respective subjects of investigation." It may be that in a true university the values of peace are not so easily come by: that "to adjust the claims and relations" of the separate disciplines, and of many points of view within each discipline, is a more painful process than Newman suggests. But that scholars should be together in the service of a larger wisdom than any one of them can compass, or than all of them can accomplish simply by adding up their labors—this is the perennial meaning of life within the community of scholars, whose chief citadel is the university.

In the third place, as I have heard the notable Princeton classicist Whitney J. Oates say so often, "scholarly work is rough," and like any arduous and costly enterprise it creates its own comradeship across the disciplines and across the generations, as one man learns that he lives by the daring and the doggedness of another. The gains that have been won and will be won do not come easily, as we shall have occasion to say to students particularly, in the chapter devoted to their concerns.

"To open the mind, to correct it, to refine it, to enable it to know, and to digest, master, rule and use its knowledge, to give it power over its own faculties, application, method, critical exactness, sagacity, resource, address, eloquent expression . . ." is not only, as Newman says, an object "as intelligible as the cultivation of virtue": it is also measurably as difficult, since it is itself a most notable achievement of virtue. "Who is sufficient for these things?" It is the recognition not only that the scholarly undertaking exacts all that a man has and more of hard-to-be-won discipline, but the recognition also that its rigors are shared by others, and that these others sustain one's own energies, that makes the university in its authentic character a sphere of comradeship and therefore a community of devotion.

All these, the heritage itself in all its richness and variety, the history with its chronicle of hard-won growth in freedom, and the joint rigors of the academic undertaking, together produce that conviction about the university's calling which is the seed bed of our present discontents. For it is clear that there is in the contemporary community of scholarship a profound uneasiness that the idea of a university is more exactly represented in the university's oratory than it is in its day-to-day behavior, and that there are forces at work both within and without the university which threaten its integrity and promise, if they are not met and overcome, to distort it out of all recognition. Many of the most eloquent expressions of this discontent have come from the works of secular academicians: but one of the most moving and illuminating of them, Walter Moberly's *The Crisis in the University*, is written with a combination of love for the university and Christian concern for its total well-being which has given the book a unique power and influence.

He elucidates the present problems of the university by paying strict attention to its pedigree. He describes with some precision the mixed elements in its inheritance, and the fact that its original character has been overlaid by elements which, though they were inevitable in their time, and have their own importance and validity, yet have never been reconciled in a coherent understanding of the university's developing nature and function.

Four Stages in the University's Evolution

Moberly identifies four stages in the evolving history of the university: the *Christian-Hellenic*, the *Liberal*, the *Technological-Democratic*, and the contemporary stage which he calls, summarily, *Chaotic*. They may be described as follows:

THE CHRISTIAN-HELLENIC STAGE

Moberly finds the classic statement of this understanding of the university in John Henry Newman, who based it on his recollection of Oxford. Here the notion of education was *liberal,* in the classic sense in which Aristotle had opposed liberal to servile. The work of the mind was to be done for its own sake, as the proper function of a man, and not because it served any ulterior, still less any practical, end. Its ingredients were to be the riches of the classical heritage, with the Christian elements of course prominent within it: but the honest intention, about which Newman was quite explicit, was not in the first place to make Christians but to stretch the mind: "A cultivated intellect, because it is good in itself, brings with it a power and a grace to every work and occupation which it undertakes." Of course the effect of such a training is to make good citizens and acceptable leaders in "the learned professions"; but it does this less by aiming to do it than by initiating young people into the best of their cultural inheritance, "the best that has been thought and said in the world," so that they become *ipso facto* that cultured elite which every society requires for the conservation and improvement of its corporate life.

Such an education, too, was *general* as opposed to specialized or provincial. It aimed at the kind of synoptic view of knowledge which would correct prejudice and breed a sense of proportion. It would do this not by initiating the student into a vast range of "subjects": that would merely make for superficiality and dilettantism. Rather it would initiate him, first, into the salient elements in an intellectual inheritance which was conceived to have its own coherence and, second, into a community of scholarship whose members conceived themselves to be cultivating various parts of the same intellectual vineyard (even the symbolism suggests that this view of the university had a strong Christian coloring!) and were therefore each sensitive to the work of the others, and to its relevance for their own.

Such an education, in the third place, was *systematic*. It could and did take for granted an orderly intellectual universe in which some things were fundamental and others subsidiary, where individual enthusiasms and prejudices were subordinated to a wisdom of the ages which was conceived to be at least the necessary undergirding of civilization, whether or not it were taken to be the revealed truth of God.

This was the university's own original understanding of itself: and who can help some nostalgia for it, in view of the dubiety and confusion which seems to have superseded it?

THE LIBERAL STAGE

On Moberly's account of the matter the liberal university defines itself by "giving a still stronger emphasis to some features of the Christian-Hellenic conception and by the total omission of others." In its developing emphasis investigation matters more than instruction, and the advancement more than the communication of knowledge. Learning is for learning's sake, but, as for what is worth learning, the university itself is the best judge, and owns no submission to church or state. "Its proper task is to promote neither money-making nor good citizenship nor holiness, but simply sound learning." To this point the ideal of the liberal university is in recognizable continuity with the older conception, and Newman himself almost explicitly endorsed it:

> I say a university, taken in its bare idea, and before we view it as an instrument of the church, has this object and this mission: it contemplates neither moral impression nor mechanical production; it professes to exercise the mind neither in art nor in duty; its function is intellectual culture: here it may leave its scholars, and it has done its work when it has done as much as this.

But from this point certain new elements begin to appear, which suggest that from now on the university will refuse not only subjection to the church as such—the older universities had fought their own good fight against ecclesiastical dictation—but to any supervening view of life which would give one study priority over another, or even suggest that one "fact" was more important than another.

It begins to be suggested that presuppositions of whatsoever kind are the enemies of scholarly integrity; and that the conditions of effective intellectual work are "open-mindedness," "objectivity," "detachment." Passion is the parent of prejudice, and prejudice the enemy of truth. Since there is no one Truth but only truths, each separate discipline must be left free to do its own work in its own way, owning no responsibility except to the data of its study, and no obligation except to bring all the facts to light. And as to what a student should study: since there can be no intention to subordinate the inquiring mind to any tradition of order that would appoint priorities, he will study what interests him, on the pattern of President Eliot's system of electives at Harvard, which was designed to insure that each man's program was "tailored" to his interests. The university accepts no responsibility now for "shaping" his mind, any more than it does for supervising his morals. He is let loose in a world of facts, to chase down as many as he has speed and stamina to capture. As to which he chooses, and what he does with the facts he accumulates: that is beyond the university's competence and increasingly outside its interest.

The difficulty with this is, however, that if the university accepts no responsibility for appointing priorities the student will have to find his own principle of choice; and since he cannot now derive it out of a tradition of "faith," he will do it by reference to the practicalities of survival and achievement.

The university, for its part, having renounced any interior principle of cohesion which would give to its work direction and selectivity, or hold its common life in shape, becomes vulnerable to pressures from within: from the imperialism of particular disciplines whose vigor and popularity bear no relation to their human importance; and from without, since in spite of its protestations of independence it is dependent at a multitude of points upon the good will of political authorities and the benevolence of financial power. The extreme of this revulsion from shapeless freedom to a surrender to heteronomous authority is seen in the Nazi and Communist universities with their subordination to the necessities either of the Reich or of the Revolution. The university, refusing to put its own house in order in terms of any interior commitment, had its house put in order for it by force of an exterior authority. In the Anglo-Saxon lands the noncommittal character of the university reflects the noncommittal character of social life generally, so that what we get is not subordination to dogma, but response to a variety of practical and political pressures, and a university which Moberly calls "technological-democratic."

THE TECHNOLOGICAL-DEMOCRATIC STAGE

The tendency here is that the form of the university's life, as represented specifically in the curriculum, is pushed out of shape by the scholarly enthusiasms of the moment, and by the demand for the type of "product" which serves most directly the dynamic forces of technological change, or the necessities of the democratic society for survival and defense. The effect is to emphasize practical and utilitarian studies, with a vast inflation of the scientific departments, and a corresponding neglect of those disciplines which promise no immediate practical "percentage"—for example, classics and philosophy (except where philosophy is prepared to let itself be subsumed in effect under mathematics). Moberly finds earlier warnings of this tendency:

> As Francis Bacon expressed it, its aim is "fruit"; it abhors sterile argumentation. It endeavors, not to storm the sky but to minister to human convenience, or, in Macaulay's words, "not to make men perfect but to make imperfect human beings comfortable."[3]

It is the scientific method which promises practical results in the technical mastery of the world, and which therefore gives to human beings the most "pungent

[3] Walter H. Moberly, *The Crisis in the University* (New York: The Macmillan Company, 1949).

sense of effective reality," so that, as Charles A. Beard puts it,

> When the great development of higher education appeared, especially in the new state universities, the secular, realistic and practical spirit became dominant, with the classics at best as a sideline. Hence one form of intellectual tyranny was escaped, not without some loss to offset immense gains.[4]

The gains are obvious: we do have immense new resources for the mastery of nature and the improvement of the human condition; yet those who are sensitive to the long tradition of the university and the complex riches it enshrines are fearful of the consequences of these new forces. For they tend to rage unchecked across the country of the mind, enlarging its boundaries, certainly, but obliterating the old landmarks, so that we can no longer find our human way about.

No one wants to renounce the gains of the scientific-technological movement, still less sit loose to the contemporary necessities of the democratic society. But the effect of the whole development is to leave the university with the legacy of its various histories, the earlier stages like archeological layers partly buried by the later. The effect is a university which Moberly calls "chaotic."

THE CHAOTIC STAGE

It is at this stage that the university community begins to be moved by a profound disquiet, which has

[4] In Preface to J. B. Bury, *The Idea of Progress* (New York: Dover Publications, Inc., 1955).

stimulated over the last period a more searching self-appraisal than has taken place in many a generation. In the balance of this chapter we shall attempt an assessment of the present stage of the discussion, and then try to see whether out of the long tradition of the West, infected as it is with insights derived out of the Christian faith, there may be resources for our present discontents.

Problems Within

Possibly the most obvious effect of the proliferation of the scientific disciplines and their activity in bringing multifarious facts to light is what has been called so often the *compartmentalization* or *fragmentation* of the university. The thing is by now so proverbial it need not be elaborated. The development of unrelated specialties not only cuts communication of an intellectual sort between scholars in diverse areas, so that their conversation is trivialized and the reality of a community of scholars dissolves away: but it shuts students up within their own preprofessional preoccupations, so that they lack any capacity to relate the facts they deal with to the whole spectrum of knowledge, still less the capacity to assess the importance of those facts for any total understanding of the human condition or the human problem. The various activities of the university tend to proceed alongside each other with nothing to connect them, as William Temple said, except "simultaneity and juxtaposition."

This tendency to fragmentation can be exaggerated,

and is already being corrected in some measure: *vide* the present emphasis on General Studies, and the other devices that we use to check overspecialization. Yet unless we can identify some principle of discrimination, some equivalent of the classical understanding of what made a cultivated man, all our curricular devices may be no better than Canute-like gestures in the face of an irresistible tide of unmanageable "facts" which swamp all meaning. And short of a new understanding of what human life is about which can set the facts in order and pick and choose among them, there will be the tendency, presently so obvious in the so-called "human sciences," to assume that if the facts in hand don't suffice to guide our action, then what we need are yet more facts: which is about as useful, as Arnold Nash says, as "suggesting to a swimmer drifting to Niagara Falls that what he needs is more water."

But at this point we are bedeviled by a legacy out of what Moberly calls the "liberal" period of the university: the assumption that any attempt to bring scholarly work and the life of the scholarly community under subordination to a governing "philosophy" is a threat to *objectivity*.

Now clearly something *is* at stake here. If by "objectivity" is meant scholarly fairness in the handling of all material of investigation, then it is a primary obligation upon all who take the intellectual life seriously, and, as we shall see, it is an obligation which is confirmed and not curtailed by Christian theology. But as the notion of objectivity has sometimes been used it is compounded of confusion and illusion. In the first place, it suggests that scholarly work can be undertaken without presuppositions, which would mean in fact that no scholarly work would be undertaken at all: because the identification of an area of interest, of a piece of work as worth the scholar's attention, involves a decision which is not derived *from* the facts but which is brought *to* them.

I recall, for example, a discussion with two sociologists about the neglect, within the sociology department, of the sociology of religion. They were agreed about the omission, and agreed that it should be corrected. But they radically disagreed about what should be the primary data for investigation. One said that he would begin by "running a study" upon the religious characteristics of Stanford's entering class. The other, a Jewish scholar of considerable reputation, could hardly conceal his derision at the notion that the religious characteristics of Stanford students were of any significant interest at all. Clearly, he said in effect, the most massive and socially important religious phenomenon in the Western world was the Christian church, and the most important clue to the nature of that phenomenon was the church's own understanding of itself. So, as the first stage of a study of the sociology of religion, he would set his students to read the church historians from Eusebius to Harnack, so that they could begin from the Christian community's own account of its nature. Now without one's trying to arbitrate between these two positions, it is patent that the decision between them represents a judgment which will determine the subsequent course of work in the field; for here, as elsewhere, since the data are limitless the work must be selective, and the selection involves a preliminary verdict about what is and what is not significant for human life.

The confusion latent in certain notions of subjectivity carries over into the classroom. For here presuppositions must direct the handling of the material, just as they conditioned its selection. It is impossible to conceive, as Robert McAfee Brown has pointed out, that the handling of the Reformation history will be identical in the hands of a Protestant, a Roman Catholic, a secular rationalist, and a Marxist. For one, it will be a true and valid recovery of authentic Christianity; for another, a perversion, not necessarily without excuse, of the true character of the church; for the third, the substitution of one form of intellectual tyranny for another; and, for the Marxist, the stirring of social-economic forces which for ideological reasons were given a religious coloration. And no matter how rigorously each may try to exclude his particular prejudice, yet since not all the books can be read, nor all the alternatives canvassed with complete impartiality, it is more just to the complexity of the phenomenon, and fairer to the student, if presuppositions are admitted and convictions stated for what they are. The notion that the classroom should be antiseptic to passion and conviction is not only a vain dream but a wasteful one, since if it could be achieved it would rob the scholarly enterprise of all vitality. The corrective of partiality and prejudice lies, as we shall see, elsewhere—in the intensification and not the exclusion of free debate.

"If we say that we have no bias, we deceive ourselves and the truth is not in us," but if we confess our bias then we have a chance of correcting it, or of having someone else correct it for us.

This aspiration after an impossible and undesirable "objectivity" is presumably the attempt to extend into a variety of academic areas the methodology of mathematics and the physical sciences. But even here the limitations of objectivity are patent. Certainly during a controlled experiment the results should not be presupposed, and any kind of finagling is not only self-defeating but immoral in terms of the *mores* of the scientific community. But before and after the experiment: in the selection of the data for study, and in the relating of the findings to previously discovered knowledge, because there is room for judgment there is room for prejudice. The notion that at this point the scientist is strangely purged of the various forms of vested interest—in established "truth," in his own truth—is a piece of superstition almost worthy of a Christian! T. H. Huxley aspired to "sit down humbly at the foot of the facts"—but flatly refused to pay attention to the new data of psychical research. The early Freudians abused each other with all the heartiness of theologians—mutually accusing one another not only of being in error, but of being in sin!

There is no point in trying to extend everywhere a dubious principle which is of small use anywhere. It would be more wholesome to admit the passion and pride, the sloth and prejudice, which infect and bedevil all our work. The corrective for them begins by admitting them, and by admitting that great as are the accomplishments and the prospects of science, this is one weight it will not lift.

Francis Bacon knew it: ". . . the human understanding is not a dry light, but admits a tincture of the will and passions, which generate their own system accordingly, for man always believes more readily that which he prefers."

And John Henry Newman acknowledged it: "Quarry the granite rock with razors, or moor the vessel with a thread of silk; then you may hope with such keen and delicate instruments as human knowledge and human reason to contend against these giants, the passion and the pride of man."

We are not yet at the point in the argument where we can propose a way to avoid the objectivity which refuses judgment, and the passion that perverts it: but at least we need not compound the problem by denying that it is there, and that for its handling we need more than the university can provide us out of its present resources.

The same problem is posed from another direction, by the demand increasingly laid on the university that it pay more attention to "values," that it equip the student not only with an abundance of data, but with the makings of a philosophy of life. The pretension of objectivity tempts the university at this point to refuse responsibility: but this will hardly do, since by its necessary procedures it does lay violent hands on those values which its students bring to it. Admittedly its essential business is to cultivate intellect and not to inculcate morals, which latter is a more massive undertaking than even the university is equipped for. But to equip men and women destined for responsibility with the knowledge which is power, and to refuse to help them find the will or the way to use it, is a species of irresponsibility in itself, and in human fact a refusal really to *educate*.

What seems actually to happen, if the conclusions of recent studies on student values are to be believed,[5] is that the student finds no help toward the shaping of conviction during what ought to be a crucial four years, and so either returns at the end of them to those habits which he brought with him, or falls victim to those pervasive cultural pressures which wait to engulf him as he leaves. The exception to this, it would seem, appears only when he meets up with a teacher of a "charismatic" sort, with something of the "contagious phosphorescence" which ought to mark the good teacher in whatever field. Such men, the studies sadly seem to say, are too rare to make a solid statistical difference.

[5] Cf. in particular Philip E. Jacob, *Changing Values in College*. See Bibliography.

Pressures from Without

The contemporary university is subject not only to these interior stresses and questionings, but also to pressures from without which may do violence to its authentic nature. Unless it can conform its life and practice to some interior logic, it is liable to be tossed about by every wind of contemporary doctrine.

William H. Whyte, Jr., in *The Organization Man*[6] emphasizes one form of such pressure, in the demands which the business community puts upon the university, and in the allure of its rewards. In 1955 the colleges and universities graduated more men in business and commerce than in the basic sciences and the liberal arts put together (and more, as he points out, than all the men in law and medicine and religion). Between 1939 and 1946, to take one statistical point out of many which suggest the same conclusion, the percentage of Ph.D.'s in the humanities dropped from 12 per cent to 7 per cent. It is probably chimerical to suggest that the universities could or should be totally unresponsive to the law of demand: but the question remains whether the university will have the bulk and balance of its work determined *for* it, or determined *by* it in terms of its perennial obligation to conserve and improve and transmit the total human heritage.

And so with pressures of a "political" sort. The "private" American universities boast with some jus-

[6] New York: Simon and Schuster, Inc., 1956.

tice of their traditional independence of state aid and therefore of state pressures. But when a substantial share of the annual budget comes in the form of government grants for government research, much of it for military purposes, it is hard to maintain that state necessities do not in practical fact condition the shape and the balance of the university's work. A university sensible of its responsibility may strive manfully to offset these pressures with the aid of private and foundation funds, but it must often feel "the struggle not availing, the labor and the wounds are vain."[7]

* * *

For the university to find its feet and keep its feet in the face of these various interior and exterior threats to its integrity, it must have more resources both of self-understanding and of morale than are presently in sight. We shall see that there are some who would resolve the matter by re-establishing older patterns, and

[7] As an amateur in administration, I have pondered sometimes, in a wistful fashion, the absence of any discussion of what might be called an American equivalent of the University Grants Committee as it is established in Britain. The situation here is immensely more complex, but is it beyond possibility that public money might be available for higher education, to be distributed by organs created by the academic community itself? In Britain the University Grants Committee, of which Sir Walter Moberly was the long-time chairman, is by law empowered to sue the government in the courts if it should interfere in the slightest degree with the *direction* in which the public money is spent. As to the *amount* of public money granted to the Committee, for that the government is answerable of course to the electorate.

some who, because this hope is vain, take refuge in sheer nostalgia. We would hope to do rather better than that, and to outline before we are through at least the lineaments of what Moberly calls the "integral university." But to do it we shall need more historical and theological resources than we have yet uncovered.

CHAPTER THREE

THE UNIVERSITY AS A PROBLEM TO THE CHURCH

The relation of the church to cultural work and cultural institutions can be seen aright only if the intrinsic character of the Christian faith itself is understood.

If the Christian faith were simply a variety of religious culture or a form of religious inquiry then it would not be so difficult to relate it to other expressions of culture or to other lines of inquiry. But the form and structure of faith is totally other than this. The charter documents of Christianity, which include the scriptures of Judaism, are not the record of human religious inquiry, but the chronicle—at least so they understand themselves—of divine initiative and activity. What the theologians call "the Christ-event" is misconstrued if it is taken to be the initiation of a religious movement, on the analogy of the insights of, say, Gautama Buddha. The Event to which the New Testament bears testimony is expressly declared to be climax and not initiation, the culmination of a divine activity and emancipation, not the inception of a new human thrust after salvation. The form of the documents bears witness to this, for the bulk of the story is in the Old Testament, the *dénouement* in the New. It is not misleading to think of the New Testament as a codicil on the Old;

or better, perhaps, as the concluding act of what Bernhard Anderson calls *The Unfolding Drama of the Bible.*[1] Its accent is not that of tentative inquiry, but of the triumphant fulfillment of hope long deferred: "Blessed be the Lord God of Israel, for he hath visited and redeemed his people." Christ died, in the New Testament understanding of the matter, not to witness to a shining new religious insight, but to fulfill a very ancient promise.

The accent of the New Testament, the classic witness of the church, concerns something secured and not something sought. It carries the assurance of a divine beneficence sufficient to take all religious anxiety away, and to free the self from anxious concern about its welfare both in this world and the next. The church, then, is not a fellowship of religious inquirers, but the New Community born of the divine charity, the New Humanity which is the fruit of Christ's death. From their new standing ground in the love of God its members trace in joyful memory the long chronicle of God's preparatory activity, to that climactic point at which the Messiah is lifted up in obedient and triumphant love to gather all men to himself, and to make a family out of the scattered communities of mankind.

The Works of Man

There are certain elements in this complex of faith which tend to determine the church's attitude to the

[1] New York: Association Press, 1957.

temporal world, and in particular to those structures of men's minds and hands which we call, variously, *civilization* or *culture*.

In the first place, these human achievements are removed from any place of ultimacy. They now can be no more than the furnishings of man's life: the vital center of it is that communion with God in Christ where the believer finds "the world well lost for love." And just as any human lover would rather be with his love in a slum than dwell surrounded by any kind of pomp in a palace, so for the Christian a certain "vanity" attaches to all the structures of the world, no matter what their splendor. Further, while the splendor of the world fades before the wonder of the best gift of all, the Christian knows also that that best gift of all was not secured by any human price, nor won by man's own power, or wisdom, or virtue. It was given, not won; and it was given to the undeserving. It tends therefore to be best appropriated by those who are poor in this world's goods, who have nothing in which to boast themselves—neither wealth nor power nor wisdom nor virtue.

The primitive instinct of the church, therefore, is to sense the threat of idolatry in any attachment to this world's goods: not to wealth alone; for power and wisdom and virtue yield so much satisfaction that they too may fill men's lives and leave no room for love.

Further, they operate to sunder man from man, since each of them becomes a seed of pride and a ground of separateness and false aristocracy. More deadly still, in the case of wisdom and virtue they become not only a ground for particular status for some men over against other men, but a claim upon the favor of God and a mechanism of salvation. In the insight born of the Gospel it is clear to the Christians that love cannot be bought, nor is the divine favor parceled out in proportion either to man's wisdom or his merits; rather on the analogy of human and parental love it tends to be partial to the needy and the outcast, those who have, and admit they have, no power of themselves to help themselves. That was why the thrust of the first Christian generation was against any kind of moralism (Pharisaism) which would have claimed the divine favor on the ground of merit; and the thrust of the second generation against any kind of Gnosticism, the notion that man could elevate himself to the divine, or nearer to the divine, by any kind of wisdom.

The same kind of suspicion attached to the structures of power: for power goes with pretension, and often with oppression, but the impulse of the Gospel is to level every pretension, to bring down every high thing, and to recoil from every kind of oppression or coercion as alien to that family temper which is nourished out of the divine love.

The closest and clearest analysis of the relation of Christian faith to cultural concerns that we have is in H. Richard Niebuhr's *Christ and Culture.*[2] The book is readily available and much used, and its full argu-

[2] Harper & Brothers, 1951.

ment need not be recited here. In effect he points out that the initial reaction of negation which he calls "Christ Against Culture" was too simple, though understandable enough, to do justice to the whole complex of faith, or to the whole sum of the Christian man's duty. It was succeeded historically by a sharp reaction, in which the structures of wisdom were discovered to have in them insights not unrelated to the Gospel, the structures of power were seen to perform notable service in saving human life from disorder, and man's virtues became a deep ground of human thankfulness if only they could be salvaged from pride. This type of reaction, which Niebuhr calls "The Christ of Culture," is represented historically by certain types of "Christian Gnosticism," and in the sphere of power by the immoderate enthusiasm with which Eusebius hailed the accession of Constantine and the subjugation, as he saw it, of the structures of power to the discipline of Christ. But neither one of these extremes does justice to the complexity of the relation between the world that God has made, for all its perversions, and the church which is of necessity *for* the world and *against* the perversions. Niebuhr identifies in the long record three other patterns of relation:

> *Christ Above Culture:* for example, Thomas Aquinas, who subordinated reason to faith, the rational virtues to the Christian virtues, and state to church, in an orderly hierarchical pattern which saw no necessity for conflict.

Christ and Culture in Paradox: for example, Martin Luther, who knew that prideful perversion infects all man is and does, and even persists within the life of the Christian man (*simul justus et peccator:* righteous and yet a sinner); so that there can be no historic end to the conflict between the Gospel and the world.

Christ the Transformer of Culture: for example, the neglected nineteenth century teacher F. D. Maurice. What seems to be affirmed here is that although the conflict between Christ and Culture is real, it is abated by the active working of the Gospel leaven in the world. To an indeterminate degree the antagonism may be diminished, the tension reduced, and the paradox softened.

Niebuhr's schematization is an elaboration of Troeltsch's *sect* and *church* distinction, which meant roughly Christ *against* and Christ *for* culture, with the former in danger always of irresponsibility, the latter of compromise. And just as in Troeltsch[3] sect and church must correct and rebuke each other, so in Niebuhr no one of the historic options is sufficient in itself, nor is any one heretical in itself. The rhythm and alternation of all five of them is necessary to do justice to the delicate responsibility of a church which must cherish the world while resisting its allure; which must bring to the service of men every resource of power and wis-

[3] In *The Social Teaching of the Christian Churches* (Allen and Unwin, 1949).

dom, while recognizing that the power will be oppressive and the wisdom deceptive, and each of them a mechanism of pride in the hands of those who hold them.

The Life of the Mind

We may illustrate the delicacy of the balance that must be kept here, and move closer to our proper problem, by noticing the particular doctrine of man which the church appropriated and refined, and what specifically that doctrine implied concerning the life of man's mind, and the apparatus and energy by which man seeks after wisdom. If the doctrine were a simple one the cultural logic would be clear; but it makes in fact two assertions and not one. In the first place, in its doctrine of Creation which is mythically represented in the Genesis story, it gives to man a unique status and dignity, not in proportion to his rationality but by the ineluctable choice and election of God. The Bible is not preoccupied with whatever uniqueness may attach to man's endowment of reason, or its dependence on the size of the human cerebral cortex. The status which it lends him—represented by phrases like "the image of God," "a little lower than God"—is constituted not by particular endowments which inhere *in* him, but by a special office which is appointed *for* him. Because of his election to exercise "dominion over the earth" as God's vice-gerent, every power of mind and hand is caught up into the context of high responsibility, to be exercised as a vocation of immeasurable dignity.

The implications of this for cultural and in particular for intellectual work are clear. If this doctrine is extrapolated by itself it means that high store will be set on all that men do with their minds; they will be the instruments of an exploration of reality in which man, in Kepler's phrase, "thinks God's thoughts after Him," and by improving his knowledge increases his mastery of the world.

But the doctrine of Creation represents only one side of Christianity's paradoxical estimate of man. It is conjoined in the record with the account of the Fall, in which is conserved the Faith's understanding that this same man, who in the divine intention stands under God and over the world in a status of unique dignity and responsibility, has thrown his existence into disorder by a radical and perverse misuse of his responsible freedom.

He does not fail of the full stature of his humanity because of the potency of animal vitality, though that may be troublesome; nor because of a weakness in rationality, though that too may confuse him. His life is fundamentally ravaged by a disorder originating in freedom (in the Will as Augustine and others have put it). And because it originates there, at that point where he is distinctly and uniquely Man, it produces a perversion touching every power and every passion. The cruel essence of the matter is that he determines upon autonomous sovereignty rather than dutiful governance, and puts those powers which were for the service of God to the service of self-aggrandizement. He becomes susceptible to lust, which is wholesome sex perverted to the uses of exploitation. And as with the body so with the mind: the power of rationality which was for the wholesome mastery of the world to the glory of God, becomes an instrument for the subjugation of the world to the service of this man. But this kind of autonomy man cannot sustain: he is in fact creature and not creator; and the more anxious he becomes in his vaunted self-sufficiency, the more doggedly and desperately he builds those structures of power and wisdom and virtue which minister to his self-esteem and hopefully may hide from him his thorough vulnerability.

In the realm of the mind, to take the most relevant example, those powers which were intended for truth seeking become perverted to the uses of self-justification, so that for openness of mind we have dogmatism, and for honest inquiry, fanaticism and the idolatry of the closed system. We shall see eventually how patent are the effects of this within the academic community itself. It should, however, be clear that with this background of belief, the church can never take man's cultural work in the sphere of the mind with the seriousness with which man tends to take himself. His truth is never so true as he thinks it is; and all his work in this area as in others is touched and tainted with perversity and the "tincture" (as Francis Bacon called it) not only of passion but of pride. How understandable it is, then, that although in certain manifestations the Christian faith has seen the work of the mind as man's best service of God, in others it has fled the life of the mind, preferring the humility which weds easily with ignorance to the pride which springs so readily from sophistication.

Probably the "solution" which has tended to assert itself, and with which certainly we shall try to operate, would belong with that point of view which Richard Niebuhr calls "Christ and Culture in Paradox." It would affirm the high dignity of the life of the mind: that in terms of man's created nature intellectual activity is the proper work of man, never to be inhibited and to be kept free of every kind of slovenliness. Yet it would insist also that in this area as in others the powers of man work havoc if they are not directed to their proper end which is the glory of God, and if they are not redeemed from being instruments of man's self-glorification to being set to the service of God. This is the true *sacrificium intellectus,* the dedication of the mind to Him without whom nothing is true, nothing is perfect. The mind is free of the pretensions of pride and the uses of self-justification only when it is garrisoned by that humility which is the fruit of the Gospel.

The Church and Culture

The relation of Christ and Culture is not sufficiently described when it is discussed only in terms of ideas, the truth of the Gospel, and the truths of reason; or even when it is discussed in terms of the several demands which Gospel truth and rational truth make upon the heart and mind of the individual man. For it is the very nature of the Gospel to bring into being a community, which is to say, in historic terms, an institution.

And since reason also in its full and fruitful operation brings men together, as we have seen, for the pooling and the mutual correction of their rational perceptions, we have a problem not only at the level of ideas but also at the level of institutions. This is more familiar in the area of power: and the history of Western society can be told pretty fully in terms of church and state, the community of love and the community of power. The state's problem with Christianity is not simply that it affirms some awkward ideas, when it is true to itself: it is that when it is true to itself it brings into being a community of a disturbing sort, which of its nature is an embarrassment to the state, because it transcends frontiers, acknowledges a loyalty which takes precedence of state loyalty, and embodies a way of life which calls all power in question.

So also in the area of wisdom. The church has been related to the university somewhat as it has been related to the state: devoted to its true interests but resistant to its claims. And the relations between these two have been as fruitful of co-operation, and as full of stress and strain, as have been the relations between church and state, for, as Newman put it, "What the empire is in political history, such is the university in the sphere of philosophy and research." And in much of the weightiest discussion of the church's role in the world, these three, the *sacerdotium*, the *imperium*, and the *studium*—the Community of Love, the Community of Power, and the Community of Learning—have been discussed as standing in a triadic relation with one another: or, if the matter is looked at from within the church, as if the church had to fight the Holy War on two fronts, *against* the claims of state and university, and *for* the true health of state and university.

The fullest account of this matter which is readily available is in George H. Williams' *The Theological Idea of the University,*[4] which is indispensable for a decent understanding of the matter, but is so loaded with scholarly apparatus as to be intimidating for those who want a general grasp of the issues. What follows is profoundly indebted to it, though it uses the material very freely, and is intended to direct the reader *to* Williams rather than to provide a substitute *for* him.

The whole massive theology of the three communities, which Williams discovers in the tradition and so carefully analyses, was developed as the form of the Western and Christian society began to take shape. As early as Pope Gelasius I (*circa* A.D. 494) the attempt began to be made to do justice to the tasks and claims of the several societies in terms of the total Christian understanding of the world. It seemed manifest to Gelasius and his successors that the functions of all three were beneficent if rightly used, and that all three existed in some sense by God's appointment. They found each of the communities—of Grace, of Power,

[4] This edition of Williams' essay was published by and is available from the Commission on Higher Education of the National Council of Churches. Reprinted from "An Excursus: Church, Commonwealth, and College: The Religious Sources of the Idea of a University," *The Harvard Divinity School* (Boston: Beacon Press, 1954).

and of Wisdom: Church, State, and University—fulfilling after its fashion some part of the total divine intention for the corporate life of mankind. Their theological rationale was not constant: for example, they sought at times to relate each of the communities to one Person of the Trinity; but they could not consistently maintain the correlation (for example, the Son with Grace, the Father with Power, and the Spirit with Wisdom) for the sufficient reason that on any sound Trinitarian doctrine God in his wholeness is present in all his acts. Possibly a more influential formulation related the life and function of the three communities to the threefold office of Christ, who in the perfection of his Incarnation had embodied the triple functions of *Prophet*, *Priest*, and *King*. George H. Williams explains it thus:

> Jesus Christ combined these three offices not only for our eternal salvation but also for our earthly welfare; only he who was fully God as well as fully man could hold all this power safely; and to save sinful man from the worst ravages of unchecked power over body, mind and soul he—"mindful of human frailty"—ordained that these functions should ever thereafter be placed in different hands until the end of time.[5]

There is profound and perennial wisdom here: that the conjunction of wisdom, power, and sanctity is safe only in God, or in Him who is Very God as He is Very Man. In human hands such conjunction can only be disastrous: both wisdom and sanctity tend to be corrupted when they are joined to power. As for the conjunction of wisdom and sanctity we must say at least

[5] *The Harvard Divinity School* (Boston: Beacon Press, 1954), p. 344.

that it is difficult and that when institutionalized, it becomes dangerous to both. So the three functions are to be forever co-ordinate but never conjoined. They are dependent each on the other in a fashion we shall more clearly see; but they are sundered *from* each other in order that each may be refreshed and rebuked *by* the others, for the total good of the corporate Christian body.

Five Symbolic Modes of the Intellectual Function

Within this triadic scheme, moreover, the particular function of the university was dramatically developed. Williams finds five symbolic modes in which the intellectual function was given status as a work of God, indeed in some sense a continuation of the work of Christ. He calls them five *themes*, which appear in the tradition from the time the university came to self-consciousness in the medieval time, were built into the Reformed understanding of matter by the work of Calvin, and were translated by the Calvinistic Puritans to the New World. These themes are, in Williams' terminology, the *Christological,* the *Transferential,* the *Paradisic,* the *Military,* and the *Critical.* Though each of these was sometimes elaborated in what seems to us a fanciful way, there is not one of them which does not have continuing power over the imagination, and which does not speak relevantly to the Christian understanding of what the Community of Learning ought to be.

Let's look at them in turn:

The Christological

The suggestion here was that the work of the mind, when it is faithfully performed, is related to Christ's own work as the divine "doctor" or teacher, who was the *Truth* as he was also the Way and the Life. There seems also to have been in it the notion of Christ as *Logos,* which as it is used in the Prologue to the Fourth Gospel seems to carry not only the Hebraic understanding of the Word of God as identical with his act, but also a reminiscence of the Greek use of Logos as that principle of order (rational order in the Greek case) which was the ground plan of the world. It is the idea suggested in Colossians I that in Christ all things *consist* or "hang together," so that all truth is his truth, and our diverse "truths" can finally be brought into coherence only within that divine truth which he embodies. This means for the university that its work is sanctified not only as the service of Christ but as the continuance of his work. It is a Christly work to subordinate the mind to the fact, to bring truth to the light that all men may be enlightened.

The Transferential

The commentators both Catholic and, later, Puritan, magnified the office of the university by giving it a part in what they called the *translatio studii.* They conceived that God had not left himself without a witness to the dignity of the work of the mind, but had committed to men in every generation the high office of *bearing* (transferring) across the generations the human heritage of wisdom. They supported this notion often by fanciful history. For example, in an attempt to gather the whole history of human knowledge within the one succession, they traced a continuity from the obscure schools of the Prophets which are associated with the scriptural figure of Elisha, to the Greek Academies, the schools of Rome and of Charlemagne, the medieval university, the English Puritan academies and so to New England. Much of this, of course, is substantial history; but they thrust also into Egypt, suggesting that the wisdom of Egypt was nourished out of the biblical world by the migration of Abraham, and joined again to the same tradition in the schools of Greece.

But whatever oddities be incorporated in the dramatic history, what the Puritan fathers of the American schools, for example, intended by it was to insist that the work of learning was appointed by God, and conserved by God throughout the generations as essential to man.

The Paradisic

This theme is of peculiar interest because it ties the understanding of the university directly to the doctrine of man as it is represented in the Genesis stories and developed in Christian theology.

It suggested that part of man's original endowment, as represented in Adam before the Fall, was an uncorrupted wisdom, short only of that final knowledge of good and evil which belongs to God alone. Man's overweening ambition to *be* god (represented mythically by Adam's eating of the tree of the knowledge of good and evil) works havoc with his mind as with other parts of his being, perverts his judgment and excludes him from his heritage of wisdom. The monastic tradition joined sensuality to pride as the root of man's deprivation, so that only by the overcoming both of pride and of sensuality could reason be in some measure restored.

> The *libido sciendi* and the *libido sentiendi* had together compassed the Fall of Man; and thus, in the monastic tradition of learned celibacy out of which the ideal of the mediaeval university in part developed, faith and continence were held to be the two ordained means of restoring reason to something of its paradistic perfection.[6]

In the Protestant modification of this, where there was no interest in celibacy nor any belief that sensuality as such was bad, the emphasis was put upon pride and its overcoming. This produced in Puritanism what Williams calls

> . . . the guarded theological surmise that, in some sense, what had been lost in Paradise by Adam's overweening grasp for the knowledge of good and evil had been partially restored in the disciplined fellowship of the school of the prophets. According to this view, the truth of Paradise as possessed by Adam before the Fall, a universal truth, had been safeguarded in the corporate custody of disciplined teachers devoted to Christ and his Church and dutifully communicated to posterity. Only in some such manner could a Christian institution of learning justify its existence in the face of the anti-intellectual implications of the Biblical

[6] *Ibid.*, pp. 303-304. By permission.

account of Adam's fall. . . . a wholesome reverence for God might be, for fallen reason, the beginning of wisdom.[7]

The importance of this for the Christian understanding of the life of the mind is quite incalculable. In the simplest terms it means—we shall develop it in contemporary fashion in Chapter Four—that reason is a dangerous instrument in the hands of men infected, as all men are, by the poison of self-love. It may be restored to its true purpose, and put to its proper and fruitful use, when the trained intelligence is incorporated in a nature redeemed from self-idolatry, and established again in humility and love toward God, the prerequisite of disinterestedness and true mutuality.

The Military

The meaning of this theme is suggested by the much-debated *seal* of Harvard, *Christo et Ecclesiae.* The notion of scholarly work as a warfare waged "for Christ and the Church" runs through the tradition, with the insistence that academic men are *milites Christi* not only when they are fighting in the defense of orthodoxy, but when they are fighting the Holy War on the front of scholarship, confounding error everywhere and beating back the darkness of ignorance. This would turn the library into a battleground and, if it got into the mind and consciousness of the Christian academician, would lend a high zest and exhilaration to all his work. But it carries also the suggestion that men may do

[7] *Ibid.*, p. 302. By permission.

Christ notable service even when they do not know whose service they are in: that any blow struck for truth anywhere and by anyone is a blow struck for Christ, and that Christians may hail as comrades in the Holy War men of reverent and dedicated mind whether they are believers in the formal sense or not.

The Critical

This is possibly the most fruitful theme of all. It depends upon the tripartite arrangement of church and state and school, but goes on to develop with precision the way in which each is dependent on the others, in an intricate pattern both of support and of restraint.

We are familiar with the notion that the church should be in some sense the conscience of the state; holding it to a high conception of its office, checking its incipient tendency to idolatry, and straightly rejecting any absolutist claims. But the church also *depends* upon the state: not only for the conditions of stability and peace in which the church can best pursue its work, but also for the needed reminder that the interests of the human community do not coincide with the interests of the church institution. The church is always tempted to test public policy by its effect on the vested interests of the church itself, at which point it is the state's business to remind the church that public policy is to be determined by general justice, not by ecclesiastical expediency.

As between the state and the university there is an analogous relation of mutual dependence: the university depends also on the state for the protection of its peace, and serves the state in turn not only by providing educated leadership in every area of public and professional service, but by holding current notions of justice under constant scrutiny, enlarging and refining the politician's understanding of what justice means, purging it of ideological bias and the distortion of interest.

But the most interesting conjunction, for our present purpose, is that between the Community of Faith and the Community of Learning. Here is a dialectic which historically has been full of excitement and not infrequent stress and strain: but the emphasis in the tradition is that such stress is inevitable, and necessary for the health of both.

Though the medieval university was unintelligible outside of a Christian society, it was emphatic that it was not the hireling of the church, but an association of teachers and students with its own inherent purpose and constitution, not to be overridden either by local church officialdom or even by the Pope himself. On occasion the University of Paris appealed to the Pope against what it regarded as the encroachments of the local ecclesiastics; but on occasion also it was prepared to defy the Pope himself, when he sought to clamp on the university the authority of the mendicant orders and their constricting orthodoxy. The members of the university threaten, if the Pope persists, that

> . . . the association will simply dissolve itself . . . they will remove the University to another kingdom, where it will have liberty; a

course which, they hint, will not be without danger to religion, since it will leave the Church in peril of falling into ignorance and of being ravaged by heretics.[8]

One of the notable defenders of scholarly freedom in those formative days, Alexander of Roes, noted the chronic tendency of church authority to usurp the prerogatives of the other two communities: "Just as the secular clergy are affecting the prerogatives of secular authority, so the regular clergy are presuming to be authorities in natural science."[9] He reaffirmed what we might call a doctrine of "critical pluralism," relying on the analogy of the divine Trinity on the one hand, and also the tripartite division of the human personality—body, soul, and mind:

> Antichrist will never come as long as the Church has the Roman Empire as a defender in things temporal, and the university of the Gauls as a defender in things spiritual. . . . Let the Pope therefore beware lest the Empire be destroyed, and let the King of France beware lest the University be broken up. . . . [10]

But what is of interest, particularly, is that out of this medieval debate came a clear recognition that the university could best serve the church by being measurably independent of church direction, just as it could best serve the state by being free of totalitarian control. It was Pope Gregory IX (1227-1241) who gave the matter one classic formulation:

> . . . if of the middle (the University) the other two are deprived, they fall into extreme corruption, because power, unless it is

[8] Henry Bett, *Joachim of Flora.* (London: Methuen and Co., 1931).
[9] Williams, *op. cit.*
[10] *Ibid.*

tempered by wisdom, luxuriates in presumption and gives itself over to arrogance, while benignity, too, if it is unsupported by knowledge, becomes amorphously degenerate and rendered akin to fatuousness.[11]

The university, then, established in its own proper autonomy, serves the church best by doing its own work well: by the process of free inquiry—this was the aspiration even if it was only approximated in fact—the university saves the church from sentimentality and also, we may add on the basis of later hindsight, from a frozen orthodoxy which claims too much finality for its formulations, and allows its proclamation to become irrelevant to the changing picture of the world which is opened up by the free and inquiring mind.

Finally it is acknowledged through the tradition, as, for example, in the *Paradisic* theme that we have discussed already, that although the university should be free of the church in order that it may best serve the church, the total divorce of the university from the church would leave the intellect to be ravaged by that destructive pride which perverts wisdom as it perverts power.

The true health of the Community of Faith and of the Community of Learning (to abandon at this point the reference to the state, the Community of Power) requires that they be free of each other in terms of power, but closely conjoined with each other in terms of mutual influence and interpenetration: in order that the church may be refreshed by new knowledge, and

[11] *Ibid.*

in order that the work of learning may be "steadied" (a word of Newman's), preserved from imbalance, from claiming more than learning can accomplish, and from the aridity which can be arrested only in the presence of mystery and by the disciplines of humility.

* * *

Suggestive as this whole tradition is, of course it cannot serve our present turn without much radical reworking.

Two things are new about our contemporary situation:

In the first place, in spite of remnant signs of the old order (like the gowns severally worn by justices, by ministers, and by professors), we no longer have the substantial form of the Christian society in its tripartite organization. All of us who are citizens of the Republic of Letters, "the universal self-disciplined society of seekers after truth," would claim citizenship also in the democratic commonwealth, the society dedicated to political justice; but only a few of us rejoice also to belong in the Community of Faith, the New Society born not out of the necessities of Culture or of Justice, but out of the compulsion of Love.

Those of us who belong in all three communities must find new ways of giving shape and vitality to our triadic citizenship: but even those of us who do not may be brought, as Williams believes, "to realize that the discourse of the university is lacking in depth if the voice of a pertinent theology is not heard." It is worth noting also his further comment, written in a time when the freedom of the university was under sore pressure from political fanatics and demagogues; that though much of this tradition may seem remote to the secular-minded academician, yet, "Upon this historic substance every American university draws whenever it finds the courage to defend the freedom of the Republic of Letters as a kind of third force, co-ordinate with State and Church, in our covenantal, democratic society.[12] Whether this be clearly so for the secular university or not, certainly, as Williams goes on to say, the church which knows this heritage will be diligent and active to defend the freedom of the academic community, whether it is threatened by political pressure, or, as can happen, by repressive tendencies developing from within the church itself.

In the second place, as we have noted earlier, our contemporary society and culture is no longer infected, still less dominated, by one single, recognizable Community of Faith. The various formulations we have been discussing were wrought out, for the most part, either in the medieval period where the form of an officially Christian and Catholic society was most visible, or in the classical Puritan period where the society was related in somewhat the same fashion, but now to non-Papal, non-Roman Christianity. If in our contemporary pluralistic society we look around for the equivalent of the medieval or Puritan Community of Faith, we

[12] *Ibid.*

shall have to accept, I think, Herberg's judgment that in the American community it is itself tripartite: that it consists of Protestant-Catholic-Jew—the three communities in their unity and difference, and in their still-normative relation to the surrounding culture.

These are two only of the factors which must go to shape the contemporary relation of the Community of Faith and of the Community of Culture. As we move now to discuss it, we shall draw largely on the tradition, but shall be reliant also on the work of contemporary theology, which happily is showing a new vitality and penetration.

CHAPTER FOUR

THE INTEGRAL UNIVERSITY

A useful contemporary dialogue between the Community of Faith and the Community of Learning is possible only because the church is finding a relevant voice again, and this not by echoing the voices of our time, but by returning to the fount of its own life, the original proclamation which brought the Community of Faith into being, which has been the means of its perennial revival, and which still constitutes the one word which has been lacking from the contemporary conversation.

Crucial Issues in the Theological Revival

We are concerned with the contemporary theological revival only in so far as it has immediate relevance to the problem of higher education. In this connection there are several issues of the most crucial importance.

1. In the first place, and in line with every classic formulation of the Faith, Christianity (in basic continuity at this point with the faith of Israel) is learning again to distinguish itself from "religion" in whatever be the general and generic sense of that term. If religion be, as Ralph Barton Perry says, "*man's* profoundest solicitude for the things he counts most valuable," then one may identify the biblical and Christian proclama-

tion as reiterating *God's* profoundest solicitude for men and for the communities of men. Specifically, whereas it is the dominant characteristic of religion to seek extrication from the problematic life of sense and time, the work of God which the Scripture records and which the church proclaims is not done that man be extricated from the world but that he be extricated from the self and from the preoccupations of the self, including religious preoccupations, and restored to that true mutuality which is the *Corpus Christi,* one Head and many members.

It is this thrust of the Christian faith toward visible and corporeal union which requires that the relation of church and world be handled not simply as a problem in the sphere of ideas, but as a problem in the relation of institutions.[1]

2. It is implied in all this that the "truth" on which the life of the church rests, and which it is the business of Christian theology to explicate, does not belong among those "truths" represented either by the cautious generalizations of philosophy, or the carefully controlled inductive truths of empirical science. Since the whole life and affirmation of the church is controlled by what it has "seen and heard," and, since what it has seen and heard it takes to be the disclosure of divine truth in divine Act, it must find its analogy for the kind of truth with which it deals, not in the abstractions of the traditional philosophy nor in the precise observa-

[1] The implications of this are discussed in Chapter Five.

tions and correlations of the sciences, but in the intensity of personal communion, where the condition of knowledge is neither detachment nor precision, but trust and love.

And since it knows that it is in the immediacy and intensity of personal encounter and historic engagement that life's crucial insights and commitments are wrought out (here it finds some affinities with modern *existentialism* whether theistic or not) it is learning to speak again in unabashed fashion about *revelation:* meaning by it not the inerrancy of any written record or of any oral word, but a truth mediated in history and community, and appropriated in love.

Though this kind of truth is generated, like all life-commanding truth, from a deeper level than reflection and logic, none the less its articulation and application—which is the work of theology—is as rigorous and demanding a discipline as any other work of the mind; more rigorous and demanding, in point of fact, since it is of the nature of theology that its work cannot be well done save by those who are subdued not only in mind but also in heart and will to the truth with which it deals.

3. One of the most momentous and relevant phases of the contemporary restatement of faith involves the rehabilitation of the classical Christian doctrine of man. Reinhold Niebuhr's *The Nature and Destiny of Man*[2] has probably been the most powerful single instrument

[2] New York: Charles Scribner's Sons.

in the structuring of a Christian *anthropology* (in the technical sense of that division of theology which deals with the doctrine of man) which has demonstrated capacity to deal relevantly with the issues raised by the contemporary human sciences, and by those deeper analyses of the human predicament which depend on literature and the drama. It is not only that bare rationalism and naturalism are thin in substance, but they leave men desperately vulnerable to those forces which tend to emasculate his will or to subject him to political or to technological enslavement. Yet it is one thing to affirm his freedom and dignity, even with passion: it is another to validate it, and to sustain the will not only with argument, but with such a mesh of loyalties as makes responsibility supportable.

We shall see that many of the dilemmas of contemporary education derive from the fact that it has operated either with the older rationalism, or with a newer naturalism, or with a combination of the two. But if man is neither discarnate mind whose distempers can be healed by knowledge, nor an organism whose problem is environmental adjustment, but has his life *from beyond* history and nature while he lives his life *in* history and nature, then it may be that the cultivation of a fully human person is not wholly taken care of by the traditional arts and sciences curriculum, the standard programatic compromise between rationalism and naturalism.

4. A theology which rests on its own essential ground finds that it need neither rush to capitulate to cultural

and intellectual movements, nor be negative and defensive about them. Rather such a theology will be an eager participant in the cultural debate, sensible of the importance of what is going on there, totally unintimidated by it, and conscious that the debate lacks depth unless it is open to the dimension with which theology deals. But it will realize that its right to participate and its chance of being useful depend not only upon the mastery of its own materials, but upon an unpretentious readiness to master the vocabulary of the debate itself. Romano Guardini, French Roman Catholic theologian of culture, states his creed:

> In Genesis God brings Adam to see the animals over which he will have dominion and to see how man will name them. We too must behold the "animals"; we must look at matter and force, at the things of this world. To this we are called by God. Our vocation is to study and know and name the world in all its categories with such depth and breadth and insight that men will ask: How is it that you see being so clearly? Then the Catholic can answer: Because I believe. That's how we witness to God today; that's how we can talk to this world about God, if we know his creatures that well.[3]

We may illustrate the preconditions of a useful Christion comment on culture by reference to science. Far from a sort of halfhearted acceptance of scientific procedures, Christian theology out of its own presuppositions identifies a special quality and dignity for scientific work and *at the same time* appoints it its strict limits.

The status of scientific work as having the quality

[3] Reprinted from *America* (America Press, 920 Broadway, New York 10, N. Y.), Nov. 15, 1958, p. 195. By permission.

of a divine commission can be variously affirmed. Two things at least are relevant:

a. The Christian doctrine of Creation. It is almost a commonplace of cultural history that empirical science has developed only within that cultural area defined by biblical faith: and that for the pointed and pertinent reason that it is only biblical faith which takes the world seriously without deifying it. Outside of the biblical world the earth is either so stripped of significance in comparison with timeless reality that it loses its interest as matter of investigation; or alternatively it is so deified that experimental work on it becomes a kind of sacrilege. But the Bible subordinates the world to man as matter, not for his rape, but for his reverent mastery: and it is in the soil of that faith that science and technology take root and grow.

b. Arnold Nash in the book on which we are partly depending draws attention to a comment of John Macmurray's to the effect that scientific work is inhibited, not only when the preoccupation is with timeless being, but when man is preoccupied with the patterns and prospects of the interior self. Macmurray identifies the change from the medieval to the modern world with Luther's insistence that the destiny of the self is taken care of by firmer and surer hands than ours (*justification by faith*). This

"put an end to man's preoccupation with himself and as a result he found himself no longer interested in himself, no longer the center of his own world. By doing this in the sphere of man's inner life Luther laid the spiritual foundations for Galileo and his successors to perform its equivalent in the sphere of man's physical life. . . ."[4]

The danger, of course, now is—and this is why the church's attitude to the work of the scientist has to be ambivalent—that we have picked up this charter of scientific work without noticing what gives it its warrant; and that we run into the gravest danger when instead of going about our scientific work with the confidence that our salvation is secured, we do it with the misplaced confidence that *by* it our salvation is secured. Instead of doing God's work in God's world, with a reverence for the materials with which we work, and a strong concern for the human use to which the results are put, we make scientific work its own justification, and are well on the way to the rape of the world.

Recent History of the University

Implicit in a theological understanding of culture is a judgment about the several "histories" of the university as they succeed one another, for example, in Moberly's account of the matter.

The Christian-Hellenic

This type of classical humanism was a massive synthesis which never loses its appeal, and is especially alluring when the times are out of joint, when the

[4] Arnold Nash, *The University and the Modern World* (New York: The Macmillan Company, 1943), p. 65.

stabilities of life crack and strain, and men yearn for a frame of understanding which will give shape and coherence and intelligibility to the world. But for a variety of reasons there can be no return to it, though it has its influential advocates who wistfully plead for it even in the presence of our galloping technology.

In fact, the synthesis was premature. It absorbed the incoherences of life too easily into the coherences, by imposing upon life a rationality which was not even the whole truth about the mind of the philosopher. It attributed to reason a competence which it has only in a qualified fashion, and was too little aware of the ideological pressures which insure that the philosopher's truth is always less true than he thinks it is. Because it found a faulty theological rationale for leaving the mind relatively exempt from the ravages and the distortion of pride, it affirmed too easily a continuity between the deliverances of reason and the affirmations derived from revelation; between the rational virtues of prudence and justice, and the Christian virtue of love. It was too confident that it knew what man is, and therefore what made a cultivated man. "Its intellectual climate is rarefied; it resembles our own no more than the pellucid air, the white buildings and the brilliant colours of the Mediterranean area resemble Manchester or Birmingham."[5] It cherished overmuch the values of stability, on the inadequate model of the city-state, and if it had triumphed permanently would have left men unpre-

[5] Moberly, *op. cit.*

pared for the deep complexities of life in which reason neither truly conceives nor fully accomplishes its ends; in which good, as Niebuhr reminds us, rides into history on the back of evil.

And it provided no real room for natural science. Its modern advocates, of course, know the presence and the potency of science: but in Moberly's phrase "it makes no deep dint in their minds." Its powers and possibilities remain "secondary and peripheral." Now we have already argued that there are some things to which science *is* secondary, but it is by no means clear that on any Christian understanding of the matter it is secondary to philosophy as traditionally understood.

There is much in the traditional view that we shall want to retain; but as a total philosophy on which to structure the curriculum of the university it has lost its allure.

The Liberal

There is no theologian of any consequence, to my knowledge, who does not regard the liberal period of the university's development as a period bringing immense gains. The older premature synthesis had to be broken; and, if Macmurray is right about the contribution of Luther to the process of emancipation and the liberation of the sciences to do their work in their own way, then we may take some Christian and Protestant satisfaction in that. We have no desire, even if it were possible, to put any kind of hobbles, Christian or other, on the process of free inquiry (we shall deal more fully with the suggestion of a new "orthodoxy" for the university before the chapter is through): but we have to accept it that the notion of an education without presuppositions is not only a hypocritical procedure, but, in so far as it can at all be accomplished, a self-defeating one. Newman was right to say that "supposing theology be not taught, its province will not simply be neglected, but will be actually usurped by other sciences." And what happens is that each discipline simply shuts itself up within the circle of its own presuppositions, or the most vigorous and vociferous of them tends to impose its authority on the curriculum, as witness the present victimization of the human and social sciences by the methods of the physical sciences.

The Technological-Democratic

If an education without presuppositions is delusive and self-defeating, it is understandable that the failure to articulate a clear notion of what, as a university, we are about, leaves the way open for all sorts of *ad hoc* decisions both by individual students and by those who shape the curriculum: and these decisions, undetermined by a comprehensive philosophy of education, will tend simply to be response to pressure. Of course, a great deal of good work will still get done, not only because of the residual strength of the older aspiration after classical culture and pure research, but because technical proficiency can be maintained only on the basis of fundamental research; and, as the cultural renaissance proceeding at the popular level now shows, men are congenitally drawn to breathe a wider air than that of the factory or the air-conditioned office.

But an inchoate reaction from technics to classics is not enough to secure the integrity of the university or the balance and continuity of its work. It remains to be seen whether Christian theology can contribute directly and positively to this good end.

The "Sacral State": a False Solution

A word needs to be said here about a point of view which appeals to certain Christian commentators because of its apparent consistency with the Christian claim. It is strongly represented in the Roman Catholic community, though also strongly disputed there, and it is probably the operative theory in many non-Roman Catholic church colleges. It assumes that the confusion in higher education derives simply from the fact that education has slipped its Christian moorings, and that the solution is to put the universities and colleges back under theological governance again.

Probably the easiest way to delineate this position is to describe first of all the parallel argument in the political sphere. This affirms that the claim to truth and finality which the Christian faith inevitably and explicitly makes, means in the logic of the matter that all other "truths" must be held in hierarchical subordination to revealed truth; and, by the same token, all institutions, including political institutions, are ordered best when they are properly subordinate to the church institution, whose *magisterium* (teaching authority) it is, which has the custody of divine truth and the responsibility for articulating it. Without such guidance human life is subject to the disorder which sin creates, and political life in particular becomes degenerate when it claims an autonomy that does not belong to it. Therefore the ready remedy for the disorders of contemporary democratic society, and the wholesome alternative to the secular tyranny which tends to replace it, is to subordinate political authority as it once was subordinated to the guidance of theology, where the true ends of human life are understood, and the political ends of man's life can be properly subordinated to his true and eternal good. The traditional name for this arrangement, which had somewhat precarious embodiment in the medieval time, is the "*sacral state*."

As late as the encyclicals of Leo XIII the sacral state was recognizably official Roman Catholic doctrine, and it has only recently been challenged from within the Roman Church. But it has been most powerfully challenged, for example, by the notable Jesuit theologian John Courtney Murray, who maintains that the traditional theory, at least as it has often been formulated, fails to do justice to the realities of American democratic life. The effect of Murray's argument, summarily stated, is that we can't have the sacral state even if we want it, and if we know what is good for state and church we won't want it. We can't have it: because the modern political society has come of age, and cannot be forced back under the tutelage of the church. The logic of single sovereignty was a politically nonadult population; and in such a situation it made sense to subordinate the people to paternal rule, and to put the ruler in turn under the benign guidance of the church. But in the modern democratic state the sovereign is the voter; and the franchise is the institutional recognition that the electorate has politically come of age. We won't want it: because the situation in which the church used ecclesiastical sanctions even for benevolent political purposes was bad for the church, an unnatural posture in terms of its fundamental character, and therefore inimical to the church's own best good. Nothing could be more wholesome than the present situation, in which the church has precisely as much influence as it earns; and in which that influence can be exercised only through the dedicated political activity of voters using their share of political sovereignty in loyalty to Christ, but asking for themselves no political privilege which they do not ask for all.

By analogy in the field of higher education, there are those who argue vehemently that the solvent for the university's ills lies ready at hand. The university is, understandably, lost without Christian guidance, and will resolve its confusions only if and when it puts itself under theological tutelage again. It is implied in the Christian understanding of life that outside of the grace of the Gospel there is no possibility of anything other than confusion. Or rather, there is one other possibility: a spurious "order" based on the worship of a false God. And this is precisely, say these spokesmen for a re-establishment of orthodoxy, what we have in the contemporary university: either the chaos to be expected when men are left without direction, or the substitution for Christian theology, as Newman warned would happen, of some secular orthodoxy. These newer dogmatisms are the more dangerous in that they do not recognize themselves for what they are: witness, for example, the statement of Raphael Demos in recent discussion at Harvard, "At Harvard, of course, we make no effort to indoctrinate." This is good for a belly laugh: but we need to watch that we do not react from the fatuousness of some of the "liberals" to a solution that has already been tried and found wanting.

The "conservative" proposal is, as in the political case, that we face frankly the bankruptcy of all solutions except that the Christian truth should have its way with the university as with other societies: that there be established in the academic community the equivalent of the sacral state. It is argued that freedom would not be threatened here: because Christian dogmatism, as distinct from other dogmatisms, has room in it for a variety of subsidiary truths, scientific and other, and also has its own built-in correctives of tyranny.

To all of which I think that the same reply has to be made: that for practical reasons we can't have it, and that for theological reasons we don't want it. We can't have it: because just as the franchise is the sign of political adulthood, so the university's assertion of its freedom from theological governance was the sign that it too claims the rights that belong to maturity. And no warnings about the hazards of the adult life will induce the university-come-of-age to tie itself again to the apron strings of Mother Church. And we don't want it: because just as the role that the church played in the sacral state was bad for the church, which is not at home with power; so the domination of intellectual life by the church theologian is bad for the theologian, who ought to know enough about the pervasiveness of sin to realize that it is as dangerous for the theologian to have power over intellectual life as for the church hierarchy to dominate the political order.

In my judgment this tempting option of the re-establishment of ecclesiastical authority in education, when it is carefully examined, serves only to vindicate the wisdom of the tripartite division which we discovered in the tradition: that church, state, and university should be established in substantial independence each of the other, in order that each may serve the other. Williams again has declared: "The University should not become a Church, any more than the Church should become political, or the democratic State take on the sanctities of a Church."

If it be alleged, as it is by some commentators, that the usurpation of the places of power in the university by secular dogmatists means that the Christians are frozen out, then the response of Christians ought not to be an attempt to capture the places of power for themselves (for here, as elsewhere, two wrongs don't make a right) but the diligent use of their rights as members of the university to build such safeguards of freedom, such proper checks and balances, as restrain dogmatic authority including their own, and secure their rights by securing the rights of all.

The Problem Remains

The option of the intellectual "sacral state" rejected, the problem remains: How *is* the life of the *Civitas Academica* to be organized, and its curriculum determined? How is it to be redeemed from the aridities of mere classicism on the one hand, and the humanly unproductive accumulation of mere facts on the other?

The absolute prerequisite is that the inheritance should not be *diminished.* That is, there should not be eliminated from it any of the salient elements which have gone to make us the kind of men we are. No transient enthusiasms, no practical pressures, no idolatrous preoccupations with the methodology of particular disciplines, must be allowed to qualify the university's total responsibility to the total heritage. Still less should any dogmatism—whether it be the rationalism congenial to Classicism, the naturalism congenial to Science, or the particular view of man characteristic of Christian theology—be allowed to narrow the options as they have been maintained and debated in man's long dialogue with himself.

In a comment on the recent discussion of the place of religion at Harvard, Robert E. Fitch wrote:

> The substantive faith of our kind of society is a faith in the specific values that come down to us from our diverse inheritance in religion, in science, in political democracy, in business enterprise, in the fine arts. The procedural faith is a faith in the kind of experimental logic which, without permitting any of these

elements to assume hegemony over the rest, shall assist at their creative interaction in competition and in co-operation. While these elements are held together in a working faith, they are not unified by any philosophy into a tidy system of coherence. Their relations are not those of sovereignty and of subjection, but are those of stimulus and challenge and collaboration and contrast. As in the fellowship between a husband and a wife it is a question, not of logical compatibility, but of a functional compatibility which shall be fruitful of further goods and truths.[6]

"What we have to begin with," says Fitch, "is a heritage which is rich and diverse and fecund." And since a "total responsibility to the total heritage" may readily become an unmanageable assignment, we may suggest two principles for the handling of the cultural materials which must be the university's stock in trade: *parsimony* and *balance*. The first would mean that the university's attention must be most rigorously focused on those commanding heights of the cultural panorama, those normative and formative "moments" which have won the right to be called momentous by putting their imprint upon our personal and corporate mind; and the second would mean that no particular scholarly enthusiasm must be allowed so to proliferate that it chokes the growth of other disciplines. The cultural debate must not be monopolized by those who can shout the loudest: it must be "moderated" by a procedure and a structure directed, on the one hand, to economy (since we can't do everything) and, on the other, openness (to all those things that we dare not neglect to do).

[6] "The Faith of a University," *The New Republic*, May 19, 1958, p. 22. By permission.

The precondition of a faithful handling of the heritage is of course unlimited free debate; and this requirement is reinforced when we remember that it is the university's function not only to conserve the heritage but also to improve it. But here again is something which is easier to assert than to validate; and it has to be admitted that sometimes the demand for freedom of discussion is more vociferous than the case for it is cogent. And I would contend that on this issue a sound Christian theology of higher education brings notable reinforcement to the case for the open university: "In this age of marked totalitarian tendency, both at home and abroad, there may be given the ancient and long-besieged citadel of Jerusalem, now receiving reinforcements, the unexpected assignment of defending the approaches to Athens."[7]

1. We shall take seriously the traditional liberal defense of free debate, to the effect that by it and through it truth tends to emerge; but we shall not take it too seriously. It is too much like resting the case for democracy on the competence of the electorate, the notion that the common reason, given the chance to declare itself, inevitably chooses well. But the case for democracy, as Reinhold Niebuhr has so forcefully pointed out,[8] rests not on the fact that it guarantees good government which it patently does not, but that

[7] Williams, *op. cit.*

[8] In *The Children of Light and the Children of Darkness* (New York: Charles H. Scribner's Sons, 1944).

it is some safeguard against bad. It is best postulated not on the wisdom of the governed, but on the unwisdom of the governors; not on trust in the people, but distrust in all irresponsible rulers.

So with the case for free debate. It does not guarantee the emergence of truth; but it does safeguard against the enthronement of error. It is the equivalent in the sphere of ideas of the democratic process in the sphere of political power. As such, prudence will suggest it; and Christian theology, with its knowledge of every man's tendency to seek more power than is good for him, and to claim more truth than is possible for him, will support it.[9]

2. Sometimes the case for freedom of the university to conduct uninhibited inquiry is asserted in a fashion close to irresponsibility: as if the university *had* no responsibility to the wider society, but was a law unto itself. But this is both morally irresponsible and practically nonsensical. The university does have responsibility to the co-ordinate authorities in the society, as we saw that traditionally it recognized in its triadic relation to state and church. Not only so, but it is dependent at a myriad of points upon the practical good will of the political and the financial power, and it

[9] This of course does not even suggest a full Christian doctrine of truth, or even a complete Christian justification of free inquiry: these would be best developed, probably, out of the doctrine of the Holy Spirit. It may be, however, that this more negative statement is most immediately relevant to the discussion on democracy, and the parallel issue of academic freedom.

simply cannot claim autonomy or profess indifference to the total good of the society within which it belongs and on which its very existence depends.

The tradition would seem to suggest—especially that understanding of the university which was developed under theological guidance—that the case for the university's freedom to do its own work in its own way, to make of its life "a thoroughfare for all thoughts and not a select party," rests not on some vaunted autonomy, but rather on the fact that the general interest is best served that way: that if the university is not allowed to bring out of its treasury "things new and old" then the whole community is impoverished, and the church and the state—along with the other orders of life—are denied the refreshment of new knowledge and the critical scrutiny which can derive only out of free debate.

In other words, freedom ought in the first instance to be granted: it cannot be asserted as if it had some bare right unconnected with the necessities of social order. If it is not granted it may, sadly, have to be fought for; but, if it is so fought for, it is not on the basis that the university in claiming freedom denies responsibility, but on the basis that it best fulfills its responsibility under conditions of freedom.

* * *

It is for a university so established in freedom to perform such a responsibility that Moberly and others use the term "the *integral university*." Their intention is to renounce, quite explicitly, any notion of putting the university under theological direction, even if that were possible. They would insist only—and that for the sake of the university's own good as well as for the particular Christian interest—that theological ingredients be included in the material of investigation, that the Christian theologian be a participant in the debate. The question is how that can best be provided for. And since the theologian is not a pure theoretician but the spokesman for a Community of Faith, this brings us back by a long road to the problem as it has posed itself earlier: How can constructive conversation be initiated again between the Community of Faith and the Community of Learning? How can the two communities, whose relation with each other has been so troublesome and so fruitful in the past, be related once again in such fashion that each is true to itself, and each is fair to the other?

CHAPTER FIVE

TEACHING RELIGION AND TEACHING THE CHRISTIAN FAITH

Subsequent chapters will deal with the informal witness of individuals and of unofficial groups related to the university community, and with the particular role of "church-related" colleges: but it is clear that the issue of Faith and Learning must chiefly be worked out in relation to the curriculum of the liberal university itself, since it is there that the substantial part of the work of learning gets done.

The Curriculum of the Liberal University

We have to develop still further such understanding of the meaning of liberal education as derives from Christian theology, and in particular from the Christian doctrine of man. And this is by no means as obvious as it sounds; for clearly a great deal of Christian comment simply takes over the liberal educator's own account of what he is about, without asking with sufficient theological rigor whether what he is about constitutes an enterprise worth doing from the Christian point of view.

There are certain kinds of education to which no such difficulty attaches. For example, technological training: this is quite clearly a particular and elaborate instance of the immemorial practice, characteristic of all societies, whereby the elders undertake to hand on to the young the necessary skills for "successful" living. From the puberty rites of the primitives to the intricacies of the modern atomic laboratory there is a straight line of continuity: here are communicated the necessary techniques of survival and improvement of the human condition, the prerequisites for the mastery of the environment. This is education with a plain and practical human purpose; it involves no definition of ultimate goals.

Theological education, also—whether it be the sophistication of the theological seminary or the more elementary business of day-to-day Christian nurture in home or church—is a clear instance of the process of transmission by which a Community of Faith keeps its faith and life alive, and transfers across the generations its understanding of life's meaning.

But liberal education is a different and a difficult problem; for since it expressly rejects the practical, and denies any dogma about the ultimate goal of man's life, it has traditionally been taken to have no end except the cultivation of the man himself, and therefore to have no end beyond itself.

We have found some reason for believing that liberal education is not in fact so free of presuppositions as all that. The practical work of education, no matter what flags may be flown or what labels may be used, requires some principle of selection among the myriad of materials available for study; and the working principle of the older liberal curriculum was the cultivation of the rational man, whose mature freedom would consist in the mastery of the reason over all the parts and passions. We have suggested already that while the Christian faith can give high status to reason among man's other endowments, it finds difficulty with a philosophy which sees reason as a cure of disorder rather than as involved in the pervasive disorder springing from idolatrous self-will.

So this traditional justification of the older "arts" curriculum is highly ambiguous from the Christian point of view. More recently, for reasons not unconnected with the crossing of the classical heritage with the biblical faith, liberal education has included a stress on the sciences, which when it takes charge of the curriculum, as it tends to do, presupposes that the mark of a mature man is not rational mastery of the self, but the manipulative (technological) mastery of the world. Just as the older curriculum concealed a dogmatic rationalism which affirmed the purity and autonomy of the reason: so here there tends to be the presupposition that the characteristic human problem, in terms of man's nature as a highly complex organism, is a successful adjustment to the world, assisted by the manipulative skills that science provides. The contemporary "arts and sciences" curriculum is an attempted amalgamation of these two, in which the balance is always difficult to secure, and tends latterly to tip in favor of the sciences.

Any understanding of higher education derived out

of biblical and Christian faith must call this whole set of options in question. It does not believe that the fullness of personal being is constituted by the enhancement of rational and contemplative power or by the improvement of environmental adjustment. On the "biblical-realist" view, according to Will Herberg,

> . . . man is a dynamic agent, acting in a situation in response to the call of God which comes to him in the existential context of life. The *humanum*, the "real" man, is the total person as a willing, deciding, acting being, and man's proper life is the responsive and responsible life of action.[1]

Now since each educational program must operate with some *image* of man, either implicit or explicit, Christian faith must be restive with the rationalism and naturalism, or the uneasy compromise between the two, which tends to dominate educational practice.

None the less, the thrust of Christian concern at this point cannot be to substitute its own *image* for the others: that would be a disguised form of theological hegemony over the educational process: rather it should be directed against every kind of reductionism which would limit the options or truncate the heritage. One obvious place at which such reductionism takes place is in the content of the accepted Classics curriculum, where "classical" is taken to mean Greece and Rome; whereas in point of fact the classical roots of the heritage go deep down not only into Hellenic soil, but into the soil of Hebraism, which was of a nature to

[1] *Protestant-Catholic-Jew* (New York: Doubleday & Co., Inc., 1955).

breed neither rationalism nor naturalism, but that distinctive understanding of man which flowered in Christian faith.

If liberal education is conceived as that process of self-understanding which is the precondition of human maturity, then it must deal with the whole tradition, for "the carrier and cherisher of full-dimensional humanity is tradition." It is in this sense, as Joseph Sittler goes on to say, that "liberal studies . . . constitute time's immemorial invitation to join the human race"—the human race not in that thin version of its existence which is all that rationalism and naturalism can offer, but the human race battered by all the problems and complexities of life, interpreted not only by the philosophers and the scientists, but by the artists and poets who best plumb the depths of the existential dilemma, and who best celebrate the wonder and the mystery of the whole. Certainly we want to hear all that a rational philosophy can tell us of life's coherences, and to be put in possession of all that science can give us of technical mastery of what can be mastered; but we shall want liberal education to give us also the prerequisite of real manhood, the confrontation of life in all its grandeur and all its misery. We do not expect such an education to come up with Christian answers to the problems, but we do expect it to come up with the problems, to expose us to ourselves in the full measure of our necessities, as far as these have been explored and interpreted by those spokesmen of our humanity who constitute its "exposed nerve."

The question remains as to whether religion and theology have a place, and if so what place they have, in a liberal curriculum so conceived.

The Teaching of Religion

Just as the demands of modern industrial and military technology may put pressure on the curriculum, with the danger of distorting it, so with the contemporary revival of interest in religion. In Chapter One we examined some of the historico-sociological reasons for the revival, and some of the factors which immediately impinge on the university—the concerns of parents and alumni, the restlessness of the undergraduate body because of its own religious illiteracy. But these various enthusiasms and anxieties are inchoate and ill-thought-out, and the university must practice the most careful discrimination in responding to them, if it responds at all. And, if it does respond, it must do so not because the pressures are embarrassing, but because they suggest to it something in the logic of its own life to which it ought to attend.

Let's take a look, first of all, at the prevailing patterns in the teaching of religion, some of which have been always with us, but have been developed both in bulk and in number under the pious pressures of the last period. Both in private and in state universities they seem to understand themselves as concerned with the study of Religion as a cultural phenomenon, a historico-sociological construct. Normally this study is housed in a Department of Religion, but in some instances—for example, at the University of Michigan and at Washington University in St. Louis, the departmental pattern is avoided. In the case of the University of Michigan a "major" in Religion is constructed by selection from an immense variety of offerings, under three heads: *Religion as an Aspect of Civilization* (including, among other things, Introduction to Anthropology, Primitive Religion, The History of Israel, Lectures in Physics, Development of Political Thought); *Religion as an Aspect of Thought* (including Descriptive Astronomy, The Living Bible, Zoology, Biblical Aramaic, Heredity); *Religion as an Aspect of Social Relations* (including Mental Hygiene of Adolescence, Sociology of Religion, Philosophy of Value, General Comparative Psychology). Washington University, which without naming names rejects the "haphazard approach, whereby random courses are scattered through the curriculum," and which also resists the notion that Religion can be handled departmentally, has constructed an *Interdepartmental Program of Religious Studies.*

> The intent is eventually to locate in each of seven key departments one teacher whose first concern lies in the two-way relations between religion and his subject-matter—what light his discipline can shed on man's understanding of religion, and how differences in religious perspective affect the interpretations of what his discipline is doing.[2]

Out of these offerings (presumably together with others) there is constructed a "major" in Religion,

[2] From an article by Edward W. Blakeman in *Religious Education,* Nov.-Dec., 1948.

but all the courses involved would be given through the existing departments: "Philosophy of Religion" in the Philosophy Department, "History of Religion" in the History Department, and so on. The overarching purpose of the program is a double one: to see that religion gets the place in the curriculum it deserves, and that it is integrated as fully as possible with the other disciplines of liberal learning.[3]

The more normal administrative pattern is the Department. Such departments vary endlessly in structure and content. In *Religious Education* (July-August 1955) Harland Hogue outlined the prerequisites for a thorough and critical study of religion as a cultural phenomenon: it would begin with definitions,[4] and would go on to discriminate not only as between the major religious traditions, but in terms also of *Primary Religion,* that is, a pure nature-religion; *Group Religion* with *its* validity and its actual and potential idolatry; and *Advanced Religion* (what is, I think, regularly called *High Religion*), which retains the valid elements in the earlier types, and goes on to develop a *deonto-*

[3] *Ibid.* There may well have been recent developments or modifications of either or both of these: I am interested not so much in the details, as in the facts that they each represent an intelligible response of a university which, under pressure or under conviction, moves to "do something about Religion."

[4] This initial hurdle might take some getting over. I undertook recently to help a graduate student in Education with a research project devoted to *Religion as a Basic Human Activity* (along with Production, Communication, etc.). After some searching around in sociological, anthropological, and theological texts for a definition of Religion we had to agree to count as religious "whatever it is that human beings do when they conceive themselves to be acting religiously." And even this could be challenged, since it is the way of theologians to identify as expressive of religious (ultimate) concern even certain professedly irreligious movements, *e.g.,* Marxism.

logical emphasis, defined as "a concern with a Universal Moral Purpose," a *soteriological* aspect, that is, a concern with evil and its cure, and a *philosophical contribution*, that is, a "reflective handling of ultimate meanings." Since Advanced Religion includes Ikhnaton, Thoreau, the Prophets, the Synoptics, the cult of Osiris, Job, and "the Christian interpretation of the Cross," I should imagine that some careful discrimination would be called for within this category. But the intention of the enterprise at any rate is clear and honorable, it probably represents on the whole the present consensus about the line of advance, and it is one more option for such universities and colleges as are determined upon a more serious grappling with the phenomena of religion.

These are on the whole the ruling alternatives, and division of opinion about them is not surprising, since the whole problem is enormously difficult. But we have to see whether we can derive out of our general definition of the purpose of liberal education, on the one hand, and out of some understanding of religion, on the other, some guide lines for curriculum building.

It is clear that, along with such interpretations of human life and its meaning as come to us in art and philosophy, and such extension of human understanding and mastery of the world as is represented by the sciences, we have a vast store of "religious" ingredients in the tradition. But when we say that, what have we said? Have we identified a new group of cultural materials which can be handled in a separate fashion by methods proper to them; or do we mean that "man's profound solicitude with the things he counts most valuable" not only expresses itself explicitly in scripture and in rite, but also tinctures all that man does—his art, his philosophy, his sexual and his social life? Is "religion" a department of life or a dimension of life? Obviously there are certain phenomena which are more explicitly religious than others; but by what curricular devices do we do justice to Tillich's saying, "Religion is the substance of culture, and culture is the expression of religion"?

The dangers with the separate Department of Religion are at least two. In the first place, for the sake of minimum cohesion it tends to settle for a definition of religion which does not do justice to the endless variety of its manifestations, to the myriad ways in which man's ultimate concern may express itself. In the second place, the religious dimension is so pervasive of all cultural phenomena, that a Department of Religion will tend to corral an unconscionable amount of material, to cover an inordinate amount of ground. By the same token it will tend to exempt other scholarly disciplines from attending to certain troublesome dimensions of their study. If everything that may be called "religious" is taken care of "over in the Religion Department"—for instance, the Sociology, the History, the Philosophy of Religion—then the assignment of the Sociology, History, and Philosophy Departments is correspondingly lightened, but their work becomes correspondingly less fruitful. It would seem to me that sound curricular logic requires that a phenomenon so pervasive of all life that it may be called a dimension of life, should have the concentrated attention of as many major departments as can bring their methodology to bear on it. If for administrative reasons a Department of Religion is called for, none the less its business should be to stimulate other departments to live up to their total scholarly responsibility, which is to deal with all cultural phenomena that are accessible to them for study, even when such phenomena bear the intimidating label "religious"; and to deal with all the phenomena which come under their scholarly scrutiny *in depth*, including religious depth. Better if all this can be accomplished without a Department of Religion at all, but if a department is administratively convenient, it should practice the most rigorous self-denial; and, since this is not the way of academic departments, it is better if the matter can be handled in some other fashion.

From this point of view the program at Washington University would seem to have the right of it; though even here there is something invidious in the notion of specialists in religion, as if any cultural materials could be adequately studied by anyone without reference to that dimension of depth which is implicit everywhere, whether or not it finds explicit expression in religious phenomena.

The Teaching of Theology

It is important to notice that so far we have not been arguing from Christian ground at all, but in terms of curricular logic. The religious depth which inheres in all disciplines—which becomes more inescapable in the measure in which they deal with man, and momentous in the measure in which they deal with the whole man—should be made explicit, but since it *is* a dimension and not a separate "area" it is best conjoined with existing disciplines and not sundered from them in a separate department. But this issue needs to be fought out with the major departments on the basis that they ought to perform their full academic responsibility, not because some pious end, still less some Christian end, will be served thereby. This point can be reinforced in two ways: In the first place, I should think it very problematic that the study of religion in the generic sense would serve any Christian interest at all. Most religious phenomena testify to views of reality which are either dubious or erroneous from the Christian point of view. Stated theologically, religion is what man makes for himself: it may be out of his fears, or in the form of projections, or (Marx) for the justification and perpetuation of existing social arrangements. That is why it is a theological commonplace to say that "religion is the prime enemy of the Gospel": because it generates idolatrous structures of devotion—out of man's needs, for man's ends. The Gospel, on the other hand, witnesses to what God would make of man, and is as critical of his "religious" as of his other idolatries. In the second place, to press on the colleges the need for "more religion" as if some Christian interest would be served thereby is to arouse the suspicion and resistance with which every institution of learning responds to pressure, maybe especially church pressure. The case has to be made in terms of the university's own scholarly responsibility, otherwise it had best not be made at all.

But no matter what may or may not be done to remedy curricular deficiencies in the matter of religion, we are still a long way from that new encounter between the Community of Faith and the Community of Learning which we had argued as necessary for the health of both. The case which we have tried to make in terms of curricular logic against the Department of Religion as ordinarily conceived, becomes a great deal stronger from the Christian point of view: for what tends to happen in such a department is that Christianity is dealt with as one variety of religion among others. And the effect of this can be quite catastrophic. Specifically the theological issues are as follows:

1. The structure of a department tends to imply that there is some generic phenomenon called *religion* which manifests itself in all kinds of local and parochial forms, of which the characteristic Western form is Christianity (in relation, of course, to biblical Hebraism). To give substance to this very dubious assertion of a generic group of *religions* which are unified in sub-

stance but subject to local variations, the inevitable tendency is to emphasize those things which the various religions have in common, and to manufacture affinities where they do not exist. The practical effect of this is that the teacher looks for some normative type of religion, from which variations can be noted: and the chronic temptation at this point is to exalt that vast complex of classical Hinduism-Buddhism which has the oldest history, the greatest numerical strength, and the closest affinity with that "perennial philosophy" which is the most persistent element in the Western tradition. To turn theologically contentious for the moment, it can at least be argued that classical Hinduism and normative Buddhism, with all their elaborations, are in fact pious variations on Platonism, the perennial alternative to nature-religion or folk-piety.

But biblical and Christian faith is simply not to be comprehended under this head. It has nothing in common with Buddhism, for example, that does not belong simply to the common humanity of the Christian and the Buddhist. What one affirms, religiously, the other denies: and what one denies, the other affirms: and this at every significant point affecting man, history, society. Nothing but confusion can follow from an attempt to treat any of the varieties of biblical faith as a version of high religion. If anything, biblical faith, the faith of the Covenant community, the historic people of God, has the character of folk-religion. It has nothing other-worldly about it, it rejects any notion of the end of life as contemplation, it has a profound preoccupation with time and history and community, it is directed not to an escape from the world but to the ordering of the world in righteousness.

2. And this points to the second difficulty that arises if Christianity is treated as a variety of religion. It suggests that Christianity is more related to and more concerned with those phenomena which are studied in the Religion Department than with those which make up the stock in trade, for example, of the departments of politics, law, psychology, or business administration. But, if anything, the contrary is the case. No doubt Christian theology has an interest in religion as in everything human: but from its classical Scriptures it learns that preoccupation with the paraphernalia of religion can be a distraction from the real business of living, which is the concern that righteousness be wrought out in every area of the common life, specifically in politics and business administration. William Temple's aphorism that "God is not particularly interested in religion" is not just a gag: it derives out of the heart of Hebrew faith, and is intrinsic to Christian faith when it is free of the infection of a nonbiblical piety.

The character of Christian theology is that it is the intellectual self-consciousness of a Community of Faith: it reminds that community of its origin and therefore of its nature, and it seeks to hold the life of the community true to its nature, and to spell out its relation to the wider communities of man. It is not, therefore, a variety of religious philosophy, but the articulate self-consciousness of the church. It has its unique starting point in the Revelation which brought the church into being: but nothing human is alien to its concern. It is not "the queen of the sciences" in the sense that it is an attempted synthesis of the other intellectual disciplines: but it does seek to join its understanding of man, nourished out of Revelation, to the deliverances of all the other sciences, working in their own legitimate autonomy and with their own proper methods. It joins what it knows of God's self-disclosure, and therefore of the grandeur and the misery of man, to what man can discover of himself by observation and introspection: and within what the "arts and sciences" can tell us of man it will detect not only precise and profound illumination, but the self-deception and ideological distortion which springs from man's necessary anxiety to conceal from himself the truth about himself. To enlist Newman's wisdom once again, it will find that liberal knowledge ". . . considered in a religious aspect, concurs with Christianity in a certain way, and then diverges from it; it consequently proves in the event, sometimes its serviceable ally, sometimes, from its very resemblance to it, an insidious and dangerous foe."

The problem of incorporating the theological ingredient in the scholarly debate which it is the business of the university to conduct is therefore quite different in character from that of incorporating in the curriculum the religious ingredients which are part of the general cultural heritage. For Christian theology, though clearly it has been colored and influenced at every point by the language and the symbolism, the conventions and the social pressures, of the societies in which it has lived and done its work, yet in its authentic nature is not a product of culture but the articulation of Revelation. Like the church whose voice it is, it is participant in and yet critical of every culture, specifically of that complex heritage which it is the business of the university to transmit and improve.

Of course the case for letting the voice of the theologian be heard in the scholarly debate cannot be based on the proposition that the Christian faith is true. The church is committed to that proposition, but the university is not. The case is simply that the theologian has things of proved pertinence to say and ought to be allowed to say them in his own way, so that their relevance can be tested by their capacity to enlarge and illuminate the deliverances of the various specialist disciplines.

In relation to the curriculum of the liberal university, as it was delineated earlier, the role which the teaching of theology hopefully will play may be stated this way:

1. The heritage which it is the business of the university to appropriate, improve, and transmit is a rich heritage—"fecund" to use Robert Fitch's word—and because it is rich it is endlessly varied. It does not embody one but many versions of what man is, and in what the richness of his human and social life consists. It does

not interpret itself, but contradicts itself endlessly. It poses all the questions, but does not purvey agreed answers: its business is to prevent the premature closing of the options, to extricate those who are exposed to it from parochial and purely departmental interpretations of the human case. It is implicitly based on the postulate that "man is his history," and that if he is to understand himself he ought to be told the whole story of his life, which is the complex interweaving of intellectual and imaginative, social and economic movements from Platonism to Puritanism, from Rationalism to Marxism. It dissects for him also the intricate structure of his interior history, biologic, genetic, psychological—all these measures which measure man at the various levels of his being.

At some stage in this exacting process of self-understanding he ought to hear the Christian witness to the grandeur and the misery of man as they are explicated out of Christian revelation, and as they have profoundly modified both his social history and the make-up of his mental and moral mind. To exclude that theological dimension of the tradition is to truncate and impoverish it, since theology has bearing, for good or ill, upon all that he can learn elsewhere.

2. If it be objected that the articulation of the faith of the church is the business of the church, then we are back at the point where we have arrived before: that for the full and faithful dealing with the tradition the university needs the church, not simply to be available for those with pious preoccupations, but to com-

ment on the scholarly enterprise by participating in it, with the resources which it draws out of its own faith and theology. To prevent that encounter by excluding theology from the curriculum is to condemn the university discussion to superficiality, since the encounter between Faith and Learning has been, in the very tradition to which the university owes responsibility, demonstrably momentous and rewarding through the whole history of thought.

3. The question of the curricular form which is proper to the encounter of Faith and Learning—where theology should be taught and by whom—is a question to which the liberal university has not yet properly addressed itself. The whole problem at this point has been obscured by the prevalent tendency to assume that all that is needed is taken care of in a Department of Religion. (The case study which follows immediately describes a pattern which may have hope in it, since it has apparently justified itself in at least one local case.) At this stage it needs to be said that it is of the nature of theology that it cannot be dealt with as one intellectual discipline among others, as if the problem of the relation of theology to other intellectual concerns were merely a problem in the sphere of ideas. Since it is the articulation of the faith of a community it can properly be interpreted only by those who share the faith and belong in the community. This means in effect that the university whose corporate mind is not dominated by a negative dogmatism at this point, may see fit, for the sake of the comprehensiveness of the

discussion and not because it yields one inch to the claims of theology, to invite the theologian to perform his own proper work within the curriculum. The theologian for his part, though he may accept the invitation as marking the end of a too-long exile, will ask no privilege at all, but will be concerned only to live like a good citizen of the university, conforming to every requirement of fairness and scholarly decorum. But decorum does not mean dullness: he can have the confidence that in the measure in which he does his work well his own life as a theologian will be immeasurably enriched by the "friction" of other disciplines, and the intellectual debate will be enlivened in so far as he can live up to his responsibility.

In some such fashion can the *studium* and the *sacerdotium*, the Community of Learning and the Community of Faith, engage again in that conversation which has been so exacting and so fruitful in the past.

* * *

A Case Study: Experiment at Stanford University

[It is not suggested that the Stanford experiment described herewith is a model to be copied. The practicalities of curriculum and the like depend always in some measure upon the structure and dynamics of a local situation, upon available teaching resources, and so on: but subject to such practical and tactical adjustments, it may be suggestive of the kind of issues that arise, and of the devices that may be useful in resolving them, when in a reasonably representative liberal university theology is taken seriously as a necessary ingredient in the academic curriculum.]

THE CHARACTER OF THE UNIVERSITY

Relevant History. Stanford University, which presently enrolls 5000 undergraduates and 3500 graduate students, has grown from the benefactions of Senator and Mrs. Leland Stanford, who gave it in memory of their only son, who died at a tragically early age. The details of its history are of interest chiefly to those of us who love it as our academic habitation and our home, but there are certain elements of the history which not only are of general interest in themselves, but are illuminating of the relation between Religion and Higher Education over the last half-century, and relevant to the problem as it poses itself today.

The University was founded under an Enabling Act in 1885, and opened its doors to students in 1891. It was established to be "a University of high degree," but there have been few such establishments in which the concern with Religion was so explicit a part of the intention of the founders, and so strongly written into the original charter. Free as it was and always has been of all dependence upon the state or upon any religious denomination, it was from its initiation free also to develop whatever forms of religious expression might seem sound and valid in a university of its general character. Senator Stanford died after the end of the University's second academic year, and, since a chapel and a chaplain had been part of the picture from the beginning, his widow shortly caused to be erected as his memorial, on a site at the heart of the campus, a Memorial Church which has since stood towering over the surrounding academic buildings. Mrs. Stanford resisted the argument that this central site should be allocated to the library, and justified her decision as follows:

> Take away the moral and spiritual from higher education, and I want nothing to do with this or any other university. I don't mean that students require instruction in doctrine; that is just what I do not mean; and it was for this very reason that I wanted the church to be and remain nonsectarian. . . . A man with an education and without morals is liable to become—indeed, he is almost sure to become—simply an abler, shrewder criminal, whose ability to prey upon society has been increased by education. Like any other force, education needs intelligent guidance if it is to serve any good purpose. And where shall we look for such guidance if we look not to the sound and unselfish principles taught by Christianity?

Governed by this conviction, she desired that the church, avoiding divisive "doctrine," should proclaim the great and uniting ideas of "God, immortality, and the moral law"; and seeking for a chaplain she admonished the trustees to "help me to find a man who will be strong enough and broad enough to fill the demands of any creed, all creeds or no creed . . . a simple follower of Christ."

So much for the extracurricular but, as Mrs. Stanford conceived it, central and crucial work of the university church: as for the curriculum itself, she deplored the fact that there was "not a single department which requires a student . . . to study subjects that will help strengthen his moral character, or help him to have and to cultivate a proper attitude toward himself and toward mankind." In this connection Mrs. Stanford proposed the teaching of "Biblical History," presumably because she understood it to be at the root of the moral tradition, and presumably also because, as "history," it would not have the character of divisive doctrine. This latter intention was not realized over the next half-century; what did happen in respect of the teaching of religion, as so often elsewhere, was that the chaplain from time to time would offer courses in terms of his interests—in one case, Bible; in another, Philosophy of Religion—but these were never developed into any substantial, coherent or continuous program.

This capsule history is significant for the general history of the American university community over the last period.

In the first place, Mrs. Stanford's high and honorable ideal was consonant with the spirit of her time: it deplored sectarian controversy in the central matters of religious loyalty and aspired after a religion which would be free of the incrustations of divisive dogma and of the rivalries of communities. It was to be a "religion of all good men," satisfying to "any creed, all creeds or no creed": a religion which by its intellectual and moral elevation would validate itself to men and women who were impatient of doctrinal trivia and enlightened enough to know that truth is not the prerogative of any one sect. The intention was honorable, but it bore little relation to the religious realities of that time or of our time. It assumed, in a belated expression of the spirit of the Enlightenment, that the essence of every matter, including the religious matter, is that the right *idea* be promulgated for the assent of rational men. It showed no understanding of the fact that "religion"—certainly Christian religion if that is the name for it—is, first of all, community and commitment, and that the life of any believing community must express itself intellectually as *doctrine,* which is not in its derivation a wicked word, but means only *teaching.* The notion that Christianity could be taught without teaching (*doctrina*) could be plausible only in a time when the self-consciousness of the religious communities had been corroded almost to destruction, and replaced for practical purposes by a well-intentioned intellectual piety which had its own demanding rigor for the best of its adherents, but actually bore small relation to the strongly articulated theology of classical Christianity. Yet how much of our campus religion is subject to the same well-meant but illusory understanding of what the issues are?

In the second place, the fact that the University did not go about implementing Mrs. Stanford's concern about religious instruction in the curriculum, or at least did not go about it with any sustained vigor, is also symptomatic of the times. Mrs. Stanford's conviction was that religion and education ought to be mixed, but nobody over the next period had any clear idea how to mix them: and there was always the strong suspicion that the mixture might be explosive. The issue is difficult enough when you talk about religion in general terms: but when you talk specifically about Christianity and education the difficulty seems to be aggravated; for Christianity cannot be true to itself without claiming in some sense *to be the truth* about life, and education cannot be true to itself without cherishing the utmost freedom in the undogmatic *quest for the truth* about life. This inevitable mutual suspicion between the Community of Faith and the Community of Learning—that the one forecloses the question about truth, and that the other qualifies and questions even the true doctrine—was itself aggravated during the early part of this century: on the one hand, by the high confidence of the academicians in the intellectual and human efficacy of the scientific disciplines and, on the other, by the incapacity of the churches to settle what their relation to these triumphant disciplines was to be. That the university administrator during that period should walk very delicately in this area, or even avoid it entirely, was not so much the result of active ill-will toward pious endeavors, as the pious tended to suspect, as the result of fairly complete bewilderment about how to do anything without doing something manifestly hurtful to the scholarly enterprise itself, which was after all his first responsibility.

The Problem of Religion. However, the problem remained, and about a decade ago, as in so many other academic centers, it became urgent, and presented itself in a somewhat new form. It presented itself in a new way because over the recent period, not only had the university itself become religiously pluralistic (the majority of students were Protestant, of course, at least in formal affiliation, but the student body included strong Roman Catholic and Jewish minorities, as well as representatives of groups more peripheral to the American tradition), but each of the communities had developed a new theological self-consciousness. As a result there was no longer even the remotest possibility of satisfying the needs of "any creed, all creeds or no creed" by an enlightened and neutral piety transcending all creeds.

This complex history produces, not alone at Stanford, a whole flock of anomalies. It can mean in our case, for example, that our baccalaureate service is conducted under Protestant leadership according to the Protestant order, though prominent in the academic procession is a practicing Jew, who was for a time the honored chairman of the Board of Trustees, and though Roman Catholic students, if they accept their church's discipline, are prohibited from attendance. Such a situation could bring anyone concerned for the ecclesiastical niceties to the point of apoplexy, but it is characteristic of American history at this stage, and it cannot be wished away: it is simply *there,* the deposit of a real history which cannot be unlived. One may console oneself with the thought that "this is America," and America has its own tumultuous way of disrupting every tidy history pattern: and I myself sometimes take comfort from Richard Baxter's great saying, "It is better to be disorderly saved than orderly damned." To deal with the situation constructively, without losing anything vital, will take all the patience and long-suffering concern that church and university statesmen can bring to it.

Fortunately the situation is more manageable at the level of teaching than at the level of worship, and it is with teaching that we shall be concerned; but, before we come to that, let me fill in a little the picture of the present campus community as it relates to the role and prospects of "religion."

The Campus Community. I have written in a later chapter about the present temper of the student body, and can be brief about it here. One of the saddening things about those—still I think the majority—who come from a background of more or less emphatic religious nurture, is that they acknowledge for the moment small indebtedness to the church-on-the-corner, though they may one day recognize that they owe it more than they know. But with few exceptions the characteristic is inchoateness rather than clarity in matters religious: and in few instances do they have a frame of religious understanding strong or spacious enough to contain and illumine the new wealth of personal and intellectual experience which is the stuff of campus life. In some cases the effect of all this is that they shuck off with some relief a religious heritage which is little better than an embarrassment; in a happily growing number of other cases they are eager to improve their literacy in matters religious, and ready for theological inquiry if the materials for it are presented at the level of their developing experience and in some relation to it.

The mood of the faculty is of particular interest, if only because it tends to show the recognizable effects of the history which has just been recounted. An untold number of them are the products of the Christian nurture of a generation ago: and it is a tribute I think to the residual strength of the Christian community, even in what I cannot but think were bad times, that an unusual proportion of administrators and academic statesmen are still recruited from those who had the benefit of that nurture. (Are there any statistics, for example, on the number of university presidents who are sons of parsons?) But in the characteristic cases of which I am thinking, the faculty man was either reared in a piety so authoritarian and constricting (fundamentalism) that he had to renounce it for the sake of his own intellectual freedom and integrity, or in a religious liberalism (modernism) so accommodated to the intellectual spirit of the times that he became a humanist almost without noticing the transition. In both groups I think there is a growing sense of the thinness of the secular alternatives, but since neither had opportunity to meet up with Christianity in its classical formulations except as a kind of antiquarian intellectual interest, they did not until recently think of it as a viable intellectual option. I heard tell of a noted literary critic, himself the product of a clerical (indeed a Presbyterian!) home, who was induced later in life, after a diligent neglect of all Christian scholarship, to hear Paul Tillich lecture at Princeton. "Why," said he as he came out, "the man's quite intelligent!"

My own sense of the prevailing mood, no doubt colored by my own immediate experience, is that there is enough residual nostalgia for the Christian heritage, coupled with a growing recognition of the new intellectual vitality of that heritage, to create among such men a real hospitality to whatever the theologian will propose, provided only that it speak to the human condition in a way that the secular options have not been able to do, and that it offer no threat to the integrity of the scholarly enterprise, whose rights have had to be asserted more than once against the church. There are, of course, pockets of convinced if not militant secularism; but for my own part I regret that they are not even more militant. The danger to the Christian enterprise in the university community over the next immediate period will not come so much from its intellectual enemies, as from the fact that it may have things too easily its own way.

THE STRUCTURE OF THE CURRICULUM

When the new mood of the post-World War II period (see Chapter One) presented the university not only with the need but also with the responsibility of "doing something about religion," the problem was twofold: on the one hand, to be substantially faithful to the intention of the Founders and to the developing character of the university; and, on the other hand, to do justice to the religious and theological facts of life.

Let me give now a summary account, with such commentary as we have space for, of what was actually worked out:

Not a Department of Religion. Those of us who held immediate responsibility for the development of the program had some initial dissatisfaction with the traditional Department of Religion, a dissatisfaction which has been increased as we have worked away at the problem. The reasons for avoiding the departmental pattern are outlined in Chapter Five, and need only be tabulated here:

a. It tends to corral an inordinate amount of intellectual territory, and exonerate major departments —for example, history, psychology, sociology—from living up to their full academic responsibility.
b. It tends to subsume Christianity under religion-in-general, and therefore does not properly discriminate and properly use the unique starting point and method of Christian theology as an intellectual endeavor.
c. It tends to suggest that biblical faith, and Christian faith in particular, is properly housed with the phenomena of religion because it belongs among them, whereas Christian faith and theology is at least as intimately concerned with the phenomena of business and political life as it is with the phenomena of piety.

d. In summary, whatever be the authentic relation of Christian faith to the university curriculum, it is not "departmental."

For all these reasons we have been increasingly confirmed in the conviction that a Department of Religion was not relevant, at least to our concerns. We have a long way to go before the phenomena of religion receive proper scholarly attention in the departments which ought to be bringing their methodology to bear on them: but this is a matter of curricular principle and not of specifically Christian concern, and we can go on working away at it. Meanwhile we have developed in another direction.

Theology for the Undergraduate. We were early convinced that the real issue in the relation of Christian Faith to Higher Education is not a problem on the level of ideas merely, but a problem in the relation of two communities. What is at stake is the reopening of the traffic and the conversation, too long in abeyance, between the Community of Faith and the Community of Learning. How can these two, which were so fruitfully related to each other in the past that each is inexplicable without the other, be related again in such fashion that each is fair to the other, and in particular in such fashion that the freedom of inquiry which the university fought for and won is not one whit abated? Of course the university deals in ideas, and theology at one level is itself a matter of "ideas." But theology is more than that: it is essentially the Community of Faith at the rigorous work of making its faith explicit and the grounds on which it rests. How can theology, understood in this sense, be incorporated as an ingredient in the university curriculum?

There was established a *Curriculum in Religious Studies* (the word *religious* is no doubt a concession to habitual usage: it is actually an undergraduate curriculum in theology), happily housed not in a department, but in an administrative unit called Special Programs in Humanities, which houses also the Honors Program in Humanities, and certain other programs which are not departmental in the ordinary sense. Without going into the tedious detail of course listings and descriptions, it should be said that in general the content of the curriculum is designed to make accessible to any undergraduate, whatever his "major," at least the elements of the biblical and Christian heritage. It includes some more general work: a course on *Comparative Religion* which was offered before the curriculum was developed, and has been incorporated within it, and a course on *The Ancient Near East,* taught essentially as a prolegomenon to biblical study. But the heart of the matter is biblical and theological work: *Old and New Testament,* both in general and in more advanced detail; *Christian Doctrine* and *Christian Ethics;* work on *Christian Classics* and on *American Religious Communities;* with some study of the relation of *Christian Faith and Contemporary Society,* and a seminar for advanced students on *Contemporary Religious Thought,* in effect a study of present-day theological trends. We also offer a course, *Christian Faith and Higher Education,* for first- and second-year students in particular, which covers roughly the subject of this present book.

This is in sum a *core-curriculum* in theology: not so very different from the kind of work that would be offered in seminary, but pedagogically tailored for undergraduates. We never did intend, nor do we now, that we should offer a "major": essentially because we have been less concerned to train specialists than to improve the theological literacy of the general undergraduate body. Initially the courses were wholly elective and they remain so, with the added advantage that certain departments now encourage students to take work in the curriculum as a departmental "minor," and certain courses can now be used to satisfy the all-university (*General Studies*) requirement. All this makes the material more accessible, but we have resisted any suggestion that it be required: partly because we cherish quality rather than quantity.

When we turned away initially from the departmental pattern, it was because we wanted to represent in the curricular structure the authentic relation of theology to other intellectual disciplines, which we took to be comprehensive and *not* departmental. In particular we hoped that we could in time win the content of specific departments to establish work of a *frontier* kind: that philosophy and history, to take two obvious examples, would co-operate in work designed to elucidate the history and systematic relation of the two disciplines—of theology and philosophy, of theology and history. Thus far we have established such work with Political Science; offering two quarters of work in *Christian Political Thought,* which is in effect the historical and systematic theology of politics, taught in this instance by the staff of the curriculum, and listed as a high priority elective in the Political Science program. We have established a similar connection with the Department of Classics, in a course called *Christianity and Paganism,* taught in this case by the executive head of the Classics Department, who is a theologically sophisticated Christian layman. In this somewhat piecemeal fashion we hope over the years to build in theological material at what might be called the academic grass roots. It can be a slow business, since it depends not only on the development of mutual confidence, but on finding men who are in effect qualified in two fields; but we have presently more available openings than we can man, and the future looks hopeful.

In any event, we have managed thus far to hold to our conviction that theology belongs with full right as an ingredient in the scholarly conversation, and that it belongs there in its own proper character.

This whole approach raises some important questions of principle, which may well already have occurred to the attentive and intelligent reader:

a. Since we have not one only but three Communities of Faith (apart from smaller minority groups of all kinds) how are their interests secured?

Two things it seems must be accepted: in the first

place, it is clear that the notion of a neutral intellectual religion unrelated to the conviction of communities does not correspond to the theological facts of life, so the only way in which the intention of the Founders can actually be secured is to do justice to a variety of convictions, rather than to pretend to a neutrality in respect to all doctrinal convictions; in the second place, as we have agreed earlier, though some of us may be committed to the truth of Protestant Christian faith, the university is not so committed, so that our right to a place in its curricular life must be grounded on the relevance (not the truth) of biblical faith to the university debate, and this means biblical faith both in its unity and variety, as represented in our culture by the *triadic* community: Protestant, Catholic, Jew.

Since by the dominant character of the tradition and the university community the administration of the curriculum is presently in the hands of Protestant people, it becomes their clear responsibility to make careful room for the integral witness of all three communities—and to make room for it, not by the way of a pale amalgam, but by way of a full-blooded articulation of the specific convictions of specific communities and the grounds on which they claim to rest. It becomes a nice question of proportion: should the participation of Protestants, Catholics, and Jews be in proportion to the weight of these separate strains in the cultural tradition, or to their present numerical strength, or . . .? I'm not certain that we have any clear-cut formula for this, though probably both factors are relevant since some practical decision has to be made; but I am sure that whatever group by the accident of history happens to control the operation, ought to put *itself* at a disadvantage rather than risk unfairness to either or both of the other two communities. In fact, we do not worry too much about a precise formula at this point: we simply try, over any given period, to achieve such a balance as we are able.

Actually we have some testimony to the validity of what we have done thus far: in that not only do we have notable and continuous help from all three communities, but we have students of all three communities regularly represented in the classes, and special funds for the support of the curriculum include contributions from Protestants, Catholics, and Jews.

We try also to take some account of minority groups outside the three main traditions, which play some part particularly in the American scene; but here it has to be admitted that the practicalities of time and staff may sometimes defeat us.

b. Should theology be taught always by believing men?

We have operated on the assumption that it should, though not without some debate even among those who share our central convictions. If theology were an intellectual "ism," like Platonism or Utilitarianism, this would not necessarily be true: but, as we have insisted so often, it is not an "ism" in this sense, but the making articulate of the faith of the believing community. As such it would seem to be properly undertaken by those who, in Paul Tillich's phrase, "stand within the theological circle," who share, that is to say, the faith of the community.

But what then happens to the university's coveted *objectivity*? If objectivity were a matter of detachment from or suspension of all conviction, then theology would have to be excluded. But we have seen good ground for believing that objectivity in this sense is both illusory and, from the point of view of fruitful academic work, undesirable. Scholarly fairness, if that is what is meant by objectivity, is to be authentically secured not by the disinfection of the University against conviction, but by the clash and conflict of a variety of convictions. Theology then, taught with conviction by those who believe it, has its proper place in the discussion as long as it contributes to it, and as long as it asks no privilege for itself, and pays regard to scholarly fairness, and to that proper university decorum which means not unnecessary and excessive politeness, but rather chivalry in battle. It cannot achieve a dangerous hegemony as long as it is subject to the wholesome check and balance of other and contrary affirmations.

c. We have had to bend our Christian and academic brains to the question: Should we take pains not only to represent the convictions of the major communities of faith, but to make room for every position on the spectrum of theological opinion—say within contemporary Protestantism? Should we painfully and carefully represent liberalism, and "conservatism," neo-orthodoxy and whatever other strains there be?

Our own hazardous judgment is that this is not only impossible from a practical and curricular point of view, but not the best use of the student's limited time, though we do pay some attention to these positions at particular points in the program. The alternative as we see it is to try with such wisdom as we can muster to communicate the classical heritage of belief, and to show its substantial modern expressions in the witness of the three communities; and if we are asked who decides what is "classical," we can only reply with all proper diffidence that *we* do, since there is no one else around to do it. But we recognize that in making decisions of this kind not only must we submit to the judgment and the mercy of God, but to the continuing illumination that comes from the ongoing discussion of this very matter. But surely, since we cannot do everything, the one thing needful is to help the student to some familiarity with the religious rock from which he was hewn, the long and strong tradition of biblical and Christian faith and life as it has shaped churches, entered formatively into the tradition, and as it helps make intelligible to him the roots of his own moral being.

d. A little further attention should be paid to a recurring question: Why *not* a "major" in Religion? or in Theology, as in the Stanford case?

As I indicated, we have a reluctance to be diverted from the general undergraduate constituency to concentrate on the training of a few specialists. When we have run a spot check on the composition of classes we have found as many as forty different "majors" represented: and it would seem that this broad outreach better serves our ends than would a program constructed for more specialist purposes. At least so it seems thus far. Furthermore, apart altogether from some increasing dubiety within the academic community about the utility of departmental "majors," we are not convinced that an undergraduate program is best organized, from the point of view of general culture, around either "religion" or "theology." Their relation to general culture is too ambiguous, and their materials, for reasons already suggested, seem best handled in other ways. If it be proposed that an undergraduate major be preliminary to graduate work toward a teaching degree, then my own doubts multiply; for if the pattern of undergraduate work which I have proposed has any validity, then the prerequisite for teaching it is a first-rate grounding in theology as such. And the best prerequisite for *that* is not undergraduate work in religion or theology, but a liberal arts degree of the very highest quality, organized, if it must be, around a "major" which best corresponds to the student's intellectual interests and aptitudes.

e. It may be of interest to some readers to consider the effect of intensive curricular work in theology upon the life and work of the extracurricular groups. Here I can speak with confidence only about our local case. My own conviction is that they reinforce each other notably. Initially I think it is true that recruitment to our own classes was secured largely through the church groups, and though now we do have a wide variety of students both pious and less pious, I suppose it is still true that the leaders of church groups encourage participation in the curriculum for the sake of a theological grounding of more substance than any extracurricular program could possibly provide. It may well be that some few students make class attendance in the Curriculum in Religious Studies the sum of their theological endeavor, and correspondingly detach themselves from study groups of a more informal kind: but I would hope that a devoted leadership would count this a price well worth paying in terms of essential nurture. On the other hand, it is clear that again and again students whose intellectual interest is first caught in the classroom, go from there to a vital identification with a committed group.

f. That last point suggests a final question of considerable importance. In what sense is curricular work of the kind I have described *evangelical*? And, if it is evangelical, how does it avoid indoctrination in the objectionable sense?

For myself I am inclined to think that clarification on this sensitive matter comes less by the development of an acceptable *formula*, than it does by the development of an *instinct* for what good citizenship in the Commonwealth of Learning means. It is clear that the classroom is not a church: there is a difference between the way in which I operate in the classroom and the way in which I conduct myself when I preach, on occasion, in Memorial Church. In the latter case I am preaching, in the old phrase, "for a verdict": in the former case I have no right, for example, to grade students by the measure of their piety. A student has a complete right to an *A* in the course for a paper lambasting Christianity as superstition or worse: the only provision is that as he disposes of Christianity he show some rigorous understanding of what it is.

The difference has to do with the character of the constituency: the church is a community of conviction; the classroom, like the university itself, is a community of inquiry. But there seems no good reason why those who inquire should not inquire of teachers who represent with conviction as well as with clarity the position in which the inquirer is interested.

* * *

The Stanford experiment is almost ten years old. It now engages two full-time teachers and will shortly increase their number, but the range of the work would be impossible to sustain without consistent and effective help from other teachers from among the university faculty and from scholarly communities beyond it. The work has been conducted, as such exploratory work is always best conducted, in decent obscurity and without any publicity that could well be avoided. I have recounted it now as frankly and faithfully as I am able, partly because I think we have made some substantial discoveries that are worth sharing, but also because I am well aware that our confidence in our local operation may tempt us to generalize unduly about problems which are in fact very various and almost unbearably complex. The wholesome ancient habit was that the individual scholar should submit his conclusions "to the judgment of the church": in this case I readily submit myself to the judgment both of church and of university.

But whatever be the fate of one particular theory or of our local practice, anything is to the good which will bring to bear on these crucial concerns devoted theological and scholarly scrutiny, and the further sharing of such fruitful experience as we have.

CHAPTER SIX

THE COMMUNITY OF FAITH IN THE COMMUNITY OF LEARNING

It is clear that a full and fruitful traffic between theology and other intellectual disciplines requires that theology be incorporated within the curriculum of the liberal university without dilution or distortion, and that the theologian participate in the scholarly debate without privilege but with that full right which belongs to any other member of the *civitas academica.* Anything short of this leaves the university bereft of an ingredient which it needs if the options are not to be limited, and if the human heritage of thought is to be canvassed in its full range and depth. The heart of the scholarly enterprise is the curriculum itself, and it is in relation to that that the issue of faith and learning must be worked out—in terms of strict theological and curricular logic; anything else is peripheral. But it is also clear that certain peripheral matters are still of high importance, since for reasons of present law, or because of a resistance which may have had some historic justification, the curriculum of many a university is diligently kept antiseptic to theology. It is true that most independent colleges, and some half of the state universities, now have work in "religion"; but it has to be recognized that it may be substantial or flimsy, and that in the vast majority of cases it falls short of being that full-blooded theological activity which the university needs for its health.

It is necessary therefore to consider the role of non-curricular Christian agencies of various sorts, which proliferate around and on any campus of significant size. Sometimes these are welcomed by a pious administration or tolerated by an amiable one; in other cases their character and variety is an embarrassment to a president and dean who are either entirely ready to take responsibility for such moral and religious nurture as the students may be assumed to need, or who do not want their shortcomings in this regard to be commented on by people who have a vested interest in such matters.

On the part of the "voluntary" and unofficial agencies themselves, they frequently operate without any very well-wrought-out theology of their function, still less any precise notion of the relation of their inherited function to the total enterprise of the university. There is therefore a vast wastage of well-intentioned effort, a good deal of irritation on both sides, and presently a somewhat feverish self-scrutiny on the part of the Christian agencies themselves.

The stark fact is that in many places and for the foreseeable future a great deal of the brunt of the Christian conversation with the university—of the traffic between the Community of Faith and the Community of Learning—will have to be carried by groups which stand in no official relation to the university, but must minister in it and to it in an informal fashion. It is therefore crucial that the work they do should be governed by a clear notion of what the conversation is all about.

An Informal History

The history of Christian concern about students and the institutions of higher learning is complex indeed; and it leaves a legacy of varied organizations whose development and mutual relations, like Topsy, "just growed." This is no place to recite the full history or to try to sort out the contemporary complexity; but at least a word or two on the history is needed to get the thing in focus.

During the earlier stages of the development of institutions of higher learning in this country, while the enterprise went forward under more or less definitely Christian governance, there was manifestly no need for explicit Christian organs of penetration into an academic community whose whole life, at least in principle, was built on Christian ground and infused with Christian presuppositions. Even after the process of secularization had set in, it was some time before the churches awoke to the fact that the student community had ceased to be a sphere of Christian nurture and had become a field for Christian mission. When this new fact seeped into the Christian consciousness, it was at a time when the Protestant communities in these United States had no organs of corporate *self*-consciousness or for common action. Therefore when the need began to be apparent in the middle of the nineteenth century, it could be met only by spontaneous initiative of individual Christians and groups within the college communities themselves, which found support from the YMCA and the YWCA. These movements had been initiated a couple of decades earlier to take care of other frontier situations lying somewhat beyond the reach of the normal mechanisms of the denominations. So the first brunt of the work was borne by student groups related to the YMCA and the YWCA, which took on the character of a national student Christian movement after the Civil War—officially in 1877.

The timing is important for more than one reason:

1. It meant that during the early decades of its development the Christian student movement, which like any student movement worth its salt is open and flexible to the intellectual currents of the time, was exposed particularly to the impact of the tide of theological liberalism beginning to flow out of Germany.
2. By the same token the movement was caught up in that tide of reaction to the abuses of nascent industrialism which began to gather momentum after the Civil War, and by the beginning of the twentieth century, under the leadership of Walter Rauschenbusch and others, was shaping the mind of the more vital elements in Protestantism with its proclamation of "the Social Gospel."

The joint effect of these two related trends was to generate within the student movements a Christian type which on its negative side was defined by a distaste for the paraphernalia of church dogma and order, and on its positive side by a strong thrust of social concern. These two impulses are still potent today, though they have never had total possession of the mind of the movements, and within the stream of Christian intention there was always a more "evangelical" and churchly element, which expressed itself early in the Student Volunteer Movement, concerned to generate evangelical enthusiasm for the service of the mission enterprise of the churches.

During the last quarter of a century, roughly since the end of World War II, the whole situation has been immensely complicated by two factors: on the one hand, the vast and continuing growth of the student population; and, on the other, the movement of the churches themselves, quickened to a new and more corporate self-consciousness over this last period, to mobilize their own resources to meet and minister to the needs of this expanded mission area. So now we have a complex of organizations related to the colleges: the Student YM and YW are still present and active, eager to perpetuate their particular genius and to build on their long experience of the work and of the problem; and the denominational movements represented along with the earlier movements in the National Student Christian Federation: the whole constituting a powerful alliance for the service of a good cause, but for understandable historical and creedal reasons poorly co-ordinated, and condemned to spend much time in discussion of their mutual relations and their several responsibilities which would be better put to the work they jointly cherish. No doubt the continuing complexity and wasteful lack of co-ordination owes something to vested interests, ecclesiastical finickiness and plain human cussedness; but there is no short way out of it, and if a way is not found within measurable time it will not be for lack of much dedicated wrestling with the problem. We shall not solve it here: but in the context of what has already been written there may be some point in delineating the nature of the total responsibility in the light of which the fate and function of any particular organization has to be settled.

Christianity as Churchmanship

We have noticed that there was some historic justification, and that there is some residual support, for the older notion that there is tension if not antithesis between vital Christianity and churchly Christianity. It was the fruit of the church's real failures, it owed something to American individualism, and it was in some part the result of theological aberration or theological indifference. This position (some would call it prejudice) is losing ground, in part because the churches themselves are showing a capacity to call up unsuspected resources of both unity and vitality.

Actually the rhythm of the church movements themselves is of much interest. In their first initiation they paid small regard either to one another, or to the older movements that were already in the field. Even if they had trusted the older movements to do the whole job of Christian nurture—which they did not—it was clear that these older movements simply did not dispose of enough strength, especially in manpower, to cope with the new numbers of students. So each denomination simply mobilized such leadership as it could find and pay for, in the first instance to minister to its own student constituency—to "take care of its own"—but with the feeling also that anything they could do as a denomination added strength to an enterprise wider than any denomination. Meanwhile the churches in every area of life were caught up into a new concern for their unity born of a new understanding of the church's proper nature, and the Ecumenical Movement, to which William Temple referred as that "great new fact of our time," generated a profound discontent with a divided witness in every area of the church's life—in missions, in social action, and in student work. In point of fact the impetus to unity at the student level had begun much earlier, since the American-initiated World's Student Christian Federation had not only transcended denominational frontiers in its own life and fellowship, but had been the fount of ecumenical concern and the prime source of ecumenical leadership for almost half a century.

So the denominational movements were hardly born before they began to explore the possibility of a united witness. But the logic of ecumenical life is to aspire not for unity for unity's sake, but for unity grounded in the truth of the Gospel: and so the effect of ecumenical conversation tends to be a quickening of denominational self-consciousness, as each community is driven to search out the roots of its own life, to make sure that in the search for unity nothing vital to its own genius will be sacrificed, and nothing vital to the full Christian proclamation.

All the movements are presently affected by this dialectic, and the immediate fruits of it are evident in a more profound theological consciousness which affects not only the denominational movements themselves, but those older movements which had resiled from theological concern because they were preoccupied with winning individual students to the Christian way, especially the Christian way in social matters.

Begging, as we must, the organizational questions which are posed by the present situation and which must preoccupy the policy makers, there is, I think, a real enough consensus to make what follows as intelligible to the whole student Christian movement as I believe it is urgent. The time has gone by when the church movements need suspect the Y's of masquerading as the arm of the churches while they tutor students in an unchurchly viewpoint; and when the Y's need to dig in on the position that positive churchmanship is the mark of contemporary irrelevance. It simply "ain't so." Tortuous and difficult as organizational problems undoubtedly are, there is a growing agreement that there must be a Christian community in the academic community which is wide open to all the traffic of free debate, but which has at its heart, accessible to all who will attend to it, a Christian witness as true to the classical heritage as it is relevant to the contemporary case.

But these are generalities. Since in large measure in many places, and to some measure in all places, the chief bearer of the Christian witness on campus must be these unofficial agencies which all in some sense regard themselves as representative of the Community of Faith in the Community of Learning, what specific responsibilities fall to them, severally or in such ecumenical co-operation as by the grace of God they can accomplish?

To Serve the Present Age

There is a growing consensus that the work of Christian agencies in the student community is more exacting than had been understood by any of them until the intensive study of "the university question" began. It is clearly no longer adequate to conceive it as concerned simply with winning individuals to find and follow the Christian way (as was the general purpose of the nondenominational groups) or to follow the products of church nurture with pastoral care lest they "fall away" (which view tended to color the first thinking of the denominational groups). The work of Moberly and others has been sufficiently influential to insure that all parties know more fully what is at stake: that the point is not to snatch brands from the university burning, but to make the reality of Christian community visible within the university, to bring the whole scholarly enterprise under the devoted scrutiny of Christian faith and Christian truth, and to assert both by word and life the claim of Christ to the service of all men's minds. To use the terminology with which we have been operating, it is to "place" the *studium* (the community of learning) in the total purpose of God: not to capture it for Christian purposes, even if that were remotely feasible, but to affirm the total obligation of Christian men within it, and to define and advance the work of scholarship, Christianly understood as the veritable work of God.

At a more practical level, it is increasingly clear to all hands that in view of the avalanche of change in which the whole work of higher education is involved, it is on the face of it unlikely that the methods that served their turn over the last couple of generations will meet the present case. If by 1970, for example, the student population in institutions of higher learning mounts to 6,000,000 or thereabouts, there is simply no prospect that this crucial area of mission can be coped with by the kind of staff arrangements which could make some show of dealing with a student population a fraction of this size. The plain fact has to be faced that professional manpower will have to be most carefully conserved, that the only way to conserve it is to concentrate it, and that the effective concentration of professionals must be, as always, with the intensive nurture of the life of the Christian people (*laos*) who must bear the heat and burden of the working day, and become the organ of loyal and faithful Christian penetration into the academic community.

It is not accidental but providential that the mechanisms for Christian nurture, which such an enterprise requires are also the instrumentalities which best serve the purpose of fostering a real encounter between church and university. It is in *Worship,* in *Doctrine,* and in *Discipline* that the university has access to the Community of Faith in its most vital expression.

Summarily the situation is this: the church owes to the university the best of the Christian heritage with all the illumination it provides upon the structure and meaning of human existence and in particular of intellectual life and responsibility. The church owes it; but it does not always provide it. But now the church for its very life on the campus, to generate and nurture the kind of lay witness on which the Christian enterprise will crucially depend, must seek out the sources of its own generation and regeneration. By the same token, by drawing deep from the biblical and classical faith which is the gift of God to his people, it will best serve an academic community which for the repairing of its own structure and the correction of its own vision needs precisely the help of those resources which are not humanly contrived but divinely gifted.

Worship

There is no area of the life of the Christian community which shows so starkly the marks of improvisation as does this area of worship. It is not only that the

Protestant community over the last 300 years in America was picking up responsibilities too fast to be theologically meticulous about the way it handled them, but the whole mood of the American community behind and on the expanding frontier has been one of improvisation. If this is true in the congregations, it is still more true after 100 years of spontaneous experiments on the campus, which are one stage further removed from any direct theological or ecclesiastical direction, and even more exposed to the pressure of immediate demands, even more tempted to action without any thorough *rationale*, and even more vulnerable to the prevailing mood of individualism, pragmatism, adaptation.

The result is a multiplicity of agencies and patterns of activity which God in time will judge, but which no man can reduce to any kind of coherence: for example, college "chapels" and college "churches," involving nice questions about the difference between them; college chaplaincies, generally understood to represent the church on the campus, but administratively wholly dependent upon the university authorities, and therefore having both the opportunity as well as the limitations of any "established" church. Then there are the Y movements in various relations to each other, to the chaplain, and to the denominational groups. There are denominational university pastors in interesting variety, some of whom do and some of whom do not have church "houses" equipped or not equipped with chapels, and variously related to local parishes. And represented within this miscellany of agencies there is a variety of liturgical traditions, and some which call themselves, a little deceptively, "nonliturgical."

Now improvisation may produce either a wholesome spontaneity or sheer confusion. Some things of value have no doubt been discovered over the last period; but on the whole we have paid a heavy price in that the strong shape and form of authentic Christian worship has been lost in a mass of inventive practices more notable for their ingenuity than for their faithfulness to Christian norms. One symptom of the fact that this will no longer do, is that those members of the university community who are drawn to the Christian heritage as providing resources of truth for life which they confess they need, attach themselves with some consistency to those communities which retain a strong liturgical life: and understandably so, since the historic liturgies at least body forth the fullness of the Christian affirmation, invulnerable in some measure to the vagaries of individual preachers or the wasteful inventiveness of those who have simply fallen victim to contemporary superficiality.[1]

Local situations vary so widely that there can be no

[1] The full picture of course is more complex than this. Some academic people, who have found the secular options too thin to nourish personal and family life, but are in no mood to return to the church communities of their nurture, settle for affiliation with the extreme liberal wing of Christianity, and find a habitation and a home in Unitarianism; while there is also an odd and unexplained appeal in fundamentalism and near-fundamentalism, especially for scientists and technologists.

formula for dealing with them. But there are some things that need to be said, for at whatever cost to cherished practice, we must somehow insure that there is made available to the academic community full access to the life of the church where that life is best expressed, in a worship sustained by the richest insights of the tradition as to what worship truly is: a worship which draws upon the whole liturgical wealth of Christendom to dramatize the relation of God to man and man to man in its range and depth, its subtle counterpoint of exaltation and abnegation, its strong and richly wrought patterns of prayer and praise.

The sad fact is that instead of this we have dismal contrivances designed to create what is sinisterly called a "worship experience," where emphasis is more on human mood than on divine activity, and students of pious inclination are pitchforked into responsibility for a function which is too onerous for them, since the conduct of public worship is an enterprise of great delicacy and responsibility, for which a man must fit himself by familiarity with the long wisdom of the church in these matters, the necessary disciplines of theology, and rigorous submission to "the whole counsel of God" as it is contained in Holy Scripture.

It is not too rough to say that the first lesson the undergraduate needs to learn about corporate worship is that he is not the one to lead it; or that if with fear and trembling he accepts such a responsibility, it can be only on condition that he lets his own poor insights be subordinated to the church's own cherished expression of its own authentic life in Christ.

To say all this is not to wage war on spontaneity: it is to redeem spontaneity from mere superficiality and sentimentalism. There is a place and time when worship should flower spontaneously; but it can grow strongly only if it is rooted in the corporate experience of the church of the ages, as that is finally nourished out of the witness of Scripture to "the faith once delivered to the saints."

Violence is done to the Christian heritage, and a sad disservice to the scholarly community, if for lack of discipline and application to the true norms of Christian worship we offer to the community nothing better than a flaccid and soggy transcription of our own poor insights. For what we owe to the university is that it should be able to breathe the high pure air of Christian devotion in a worship in which every human enterprise, including the academic enterprise, is seen in true perspective by being related to God's strong governance of the world, and in which every human failure, including the sin that so easily besets the academic man, is transmuted by the divine forgiveness to become a fulcrum for the work of grace and renewal.

Doctrine

Any student movement, by virtue of the fact that it *is* a student movement, is accessible to the intellectual currents of any given time: it is vulnerable to every kind of extremism, and by the same token tends to feel the impact of any theological movement of recovery earlier and more violently than does the main body of the church. This exposure to the oscillation of Christian and cultural trends is inevitable in the nature of the case: it is simply one of the occupational hazards of being part of the intellectual community, not to be lamented but simply understood. There can be no hope and no health in any attempt to hold the pendulum steady, or to restrict the range of inquiry. The discussion will and ought to range as widely as the available options; but what needs to be insured is that as all the options are canvassed and every outrageous opinion is weighed, there be available, at least as an ingredient in the discussion, a responsible statement of the classical Christian faith in those great and normative and church-shaping statements of it which are so rich a part of the Christian heritage.

From this point of view it has to be confessed that much of the work of the unofficial groups has been sadly lacking in theological substance. In this sphere as in that of worship, we owe to the university this at least: that we make available to it for examination the best of the Christian heritage in thought and *doctrine* (a word which used to be avoided, but means simply, when we look squarely at it, *doctrina:* teaching). The subjectivism of the last period has meant that almost as a matter of principle we have felt bound to "begin where students are," and to "follow their interests." This tends to lead to frustration, for the simple reason that students on the whole don't know where they are:

and the attempt to follow their interests, which are narrow in range and endlessly fluctuating in content, means an *ad hoc* program of topics for discussion which add up to no coherent understanding either of the Christian faith or of anything else.

There are several signs of hope in the present situation. In the first place, there is a general recognition of the fact that students grow tired of tramping round within the circle of their own preoccupations, that simply to pool student insights will solve no student problems, because most problems require for their "solution" that they be set within a much wider frame of Christian understanding than any one generation, still less any group within one generation, can command. I can illustrate this, I think. I do a good deal of itinerating on the campuses, and I begin to notice a difference in the character of the invitation. Time was when it came in somewhat this form: "Could you come to such-and-such a campus on such-and-such a night to talk to the ——— group?" "Well, I think I can make the date all right, but what do you want me to talk about?" "Oh, anything you like, really. . . ." And I had the despairing feeling that I was talking to a program secretary who had the responsibility simply for filling a given number of evenings with a set of reasonably respectable "topics" by a set of reasonably reputable speakers. I make it a rule now not to take that kind of invitation, but on the whole I don't have to: because more and more I notice that the approach is rather like this: "Mr. Miller, during the first semester we are studying The Christian Doctrine of Man, and we're reading Niebuhr (or Brunner or. . .). Could you lead the discussion on The Fall, or on what Justification by Faith means?" This kind of invitation I rejoice to take, because it sounds as if I might be contributing what I think is my valuable time at least to a study project that is getting somewhere. In the second place, this increasing seriousness is matched by increasing resources out of the contemporary theological revival which are set down in contemporary terms, but which are in some recognizable continuity with the great and formative figures in the tradition, and are explicitly indebted in the end of the day to the Bible itself.

There is a good deal of ground still to be gained. It is good that attempts are increasingly being made to bring noncurricular work on to some kind of approximate parity with the curriculum—which means not only quality but some kind of continuity. And the more responsible movements are increasingly managing to recruit to their professional staffs men and women who hold academic qualifications which enable them to participate in the scholarly debate and to move with some ease in the scholarly community. Purity of life will always matter more than intellectual sophistication, but for this specialist operation we especially need to add to our faith knowledge. So far, so good: but much of our work is still a shambles if measured by any real yardstick of scholarly responsibility. Could we not, for example, devise ways out of our joint resources of providing for each campus community a curriculum of study which over four years would cover with reasonable adequacy the main subject matter of Christian and biblical theology: say, the Bible in one year, Systematic Theology one year, the third year Christian Ethics, and possibly a rather free-ranging discussion of Christ and Culture in the fourth year. This is only one of a number of options and may not be the best one.

In a relatively large university we have found it possible and useful to offer a number of options each year; but the main intention is clear—to make it possible for a student through his or her four years to undertake a program of study which has both depth and continuity to it, and to come out at the end with both the satisfaction of real achievement and the reward of real and substantial knowledge of the Christian faith, the grounds on which it rests, and its relevance to a variety of personal, social, and cultural questions. Of course such a program need not be inflexible: there is room within it and around it for any number of episodic and immediate questions, but the enterprise of Christian inquiry should be in a frame large enough to make room for the range of Christian truth, and strong enough to hold it in shape.

So with the various tried-and-true devices, used by all the movements, of camp and conference and "retreat." The device itself is admirable, but the content is too often flimsy and ephemeral. The themes are too general and not massive or concentrated enough. *Christ and Our World* might mean anything or nothing: it means ordinarily a somewhat scattered and disorderly discussion of things in general. It is time that students discovered—they have tried almost everything else—that there can be far more illumination and exhilaration from grappling with a really seminal piece of thinking, a piece of work which has proved itself strong and durable enough to make and break churches, and to be a continuing resource for Christian reflection through many a generation: too many of our groups are denied the chance to discover how rewarding could be *A Week End with Luther*—say, on the basis of *The Treatise on Christian Liberty*, or a full week with Newman's *The Idea of a University*, which has more theological and intellectual substance and excitement to it than goes into many a four-year drudgery of patchwork programs. Works of this stature are pouring now from the paperback presses. Since someone must be reading them, it is a gross deprivation if they are not made available through the normal operation of our committed Christian groups.

However, whatever be the details of the strategy, the intent should be that the Christian community of witness and the university community of inquiry should have at its heart the organism of Christian truth strongly articulated and not emasculated. The honest inquirer may or may not buy it (the metaphor begins to be mixed) but he should know what it is.

Discipline

Like the word *doctrine*, this word may create an initial recoil in those whose instinct is libertarian; but it means only *discipleship,* and in the present context it concerns the corporate life of the witnessing community in the college and university.

How is the quality of its life to be measured, and how far does its effective witness *depend* upon the quality of its life? We shall have much to say in Chapter Eight about the specific obligations of Christian citizenship in the Commonwealth of Letters, but the point here is the common life of the Christian group *as* a Christian group, whatever its label.

The triadic expression in *worship, doctrine,* and *discipline* is traditionally descriptive of the life of the church—but in some sense these three phases must be present wherever and however informally the Community of Faith is represented, and where Christ is sought to be served with heart and mind and will.

Discipline in the first instance has nothing to do with rigor, still less with rigidity: it has to do with quality. And the impact of the Christian witness upon the wider world will always have a good deal more to do with quality of life than with loquacity, plausibility of argument, or even theological precision, important as this latter is. Under this head there are some things so trite they need hardly be stated, though they are trite only in that they are basic: that the community of faith should be, according to its nature, inclusive of every group especially those groups that are normally disadvantaged, say by race or by color; that the community should be hospitable to the "despised and rejected" of the society, welcoming with unpretentious and unself-conscious warmth those who lack the graces which make for instant popularity in a society which lives by phoney status symbols.

These interior marks of the committed community are clear, and there are others. But vital also is the capacity of the community to generate a disinterested concern for the health of that society—in this case the academic community—in which its life is set. To it nothing human, and in this case nothing intellectual, should be alien: curricular structure, university and student government, the necessary guarantees of academic freedom, the patterns of residence which tell for or against the free flow of scholarly discussion, and the free traffic of such variety of social groups as may be present to enrich each other. The health of the Christian community will be measured less by the multiplicity of its own official activities, than by the unobtrusive presence and activity of its members at every strategic center of university life.

And its disinterested activity is not limited by the frontiers of the campus. It will be aware because of its own world-wide affiliation how easily the campus operates to insulate from contemporary crisis and to exonerate from contemporary decision; and it will function, by a well-cultivated humane imagination, as a sort of exposed nerve of the university community, vibrating to the tragic movement of the multitudes of men across a distraught and desperately needy world.

CHAPTER SEVEN

THE VOCATION OF THE CHRISTIAN COLLEGE

We discovered earlier that in the nature of the case the relation between Faith and Culture, and therefore between the Community of Faith and the Community of Learning, must always have elements of tension in it, tension which, if properly understood and rightly handled, can be of profit to both. But the relation becomes more exacting, and potentially it may be even more rewarding, when these two communities by the "accident" of history come to live as it were under the same roof.

Something specific therefore needs to be said about the Christian or "church-related" college, which is so characteristic a part of the American educational scene. Virtually my only qualification for trying to say it is that I spent a strenuous and rewarding year in intimate participation in the discussions leading to the Second Quadrennial Convocation of Christian Colleges which was held at Drake University in June, 1958. I had a hand also in the deliberations of the Convocation itself, which produced a mass of important and available material,[1] but which, as is the way with convoca-

[1] "The Vocation of a Christian College," *The Christian Scholar*, Vol. XLI, Autumn, 1958.

tions, nowhere precisely reproduced the view of any one participant, specifically, in this case, mine. So for what it is worth I propose now to set out at least the elements of that view of the Christian colleges which would seem to be consistent with what has been said thus far. It is indebted to the discussions that went on in and around the Convocation, it probably lacks the comprehensive and balanced wisdom of the deliverances of the Convocation, but by the same token may have more argumentative point and pungency to it.

I propose, for reasons both of theology and of semantic convenience, to use the term "Christian college" to refer to any institution of higher learning for which the church (which means for present and practical purposes any one of the Protestant churches) retains any significant measure of responsibility. The convenience of this terminology is obvious; the theological reason for it may be illustrated by a true chronicle. I went recently to visit one of the better of our denominational colleges, to discuss with faculty and students over a number of days the theme, "Is ——— a Christian college?" I took a line which seemed to me, from an historical and theological point of view, obvious. I pointed out that the term "Christian" in its origin and consistent usage, refers not to some measure of moral or spiritual achievement (if it did, who would judge whom? And how much morality or spirituality—51 per cent?—would be required to "rate" as Christian?), but to visible identification, normally by the sign of Baptism, with a visible Community. In the case of individuals in their relation to the church, this means that all baptized persons are Christians (presumably, unless they formally renounce their baptism), but it acknowledges that within this very mixed company are Christians both good, bad, and indifferent—none of them perfect, none of them, hopefully, totally beyond hope. By analogy this would mean that when we ask about the Christianity of a college, we are not undertaking the impossible chore of assessing its morality or spirituality: we are asking simply if it is "baptized"—that is, if it is visibly and formally related to the church. Since in this particular case the church-relation was undeniable and indeed insisted on, I proposed that we accept the fact that ——— College was Christian by virtue of its "baptism" and that we then ask in plain terms what ought to be going on there: and I began by insisting that since ——— College was a Christian college, what ought first of all to be going on there was the full performance of a first-rate intellectual enterprise, the conduct of academic life to the glory and praise of God. The sequel was illuminating, though not directly to the present point. As soon as the lecture was over, I was approached by a somewhat anxious group of students who asserted that I had totally misunderstood their problem: which was whether ——— College was a *Christian* college. "You see," they said, "some people say it isn't. And they complain especially about our yells . . . one of which is SEX! RAH! and another of which has a swear-word in it." I collected myself enough to suggest that since God had made sex he probably wouldn't mind people's cheering it; and that whatever were the criteria for a Christian college, they probably had more to do with what the college did in its work time, than with what it didn't do in its spare time. But I was left with some somber reflections about the use of moralistic categories for discussion of what is far from being a moralistic issue.

At least this horror-story is justified in the long telling since it suggests that we need to get the whole matter in fuller and truer theological and historical focus if we are to make sense of the present dilemma of the Christian college.

The Elements of the History

The settlers of New England brought to this land an inherited concern for learning. Having established the ordinances of worship and set up the apparatus of civil government, they took care "to advance learning and perpetuate it to posterity, dreading to leave an illiterate ministry to the churches." Though their explicit concern was for a learned ministry, they were, in practice, in line with the long tradition, which took the universities to be the nursery of leadership for the church and for the state, for the university itself, and for the professional classes. As the frontier moved westward, these concerns moved along with it, and colleges appeared behind the frontier with regularity and in great profusion. In the nature of the case they were under the aegis of the church, for only the church had sufficient vitality and sufficient stability to undertake the work. So by the time of the Civil War more than 500 colleges, generally church-sponsored, existed in sixteen states.

In this as in other areas of American life the frontier was almost a synonym for improvisation: and it seems clear that throughout this development there was in the nature of the case more practice than theory, so much activity in the field of education that there was small time to develop a theology of what was going on. The overriding consideration was to get the work of education done; and some denominations, especially the more conservative of them, were interested in having the work of education conducted under church tutelage so that the young people of the churches be secured against the tendency to heterodoxy always latent in intellectual activity.

The facts of the situation, nevertheless, as might have been expected, determined that even within the close-quarters relationship of church and college in the church college, the dynamic of faith and learning would express itself in stress and strain: indeed, the fact that the Community of Faith and the Community of Learning had for reasons of historic necessity come to live under one roof, made the stress even more onerous.

In general there were three possible issues of the matter; and each one of them is represented among the variety of situations with which we now have to deal:

1. Certain of the more conservative denominations simply clamped firm theological control upon the educational process in their schools, with doctrinal tests for teachers, the elimination of "dangerous" material from the curriculum, and so on.

2. In other instances, indeed a significant number, the college simply sailed off on the sea of intellectual inquiry, gathering momentum by recruiting both students and support from outside the immediate church constituency, filling its sails with the wind of various doctrines—in all these ways being true to its nature as a community of free inquiry, and ending as a liberal university in the generic sense, its relations with the church either tenuous or nonexistent.

3. Others retained a more substantial church connection and some claim to church support by a compromise between faith and liberal learning which took the form of an emphasis on "character"—"a virtue," as David Riesman says, "on which classicists and the devout could agree." This means in effect the end of any theological undergirding for the scholarly enterprise, and a scrutiny of the catalogues of Christian colleges now turns up with monotonous frequency what Joseph Sittler calls "the melancholy statement" that the aim of the college is the cultivation of "moral and spiritual values." In practice these turn out to be in effect the ruling *mores* of the American middle-class community, but this emphasis enables the Christian colleges to make some claim to special regard amid the proliferation of state and municipal institutions, which,

though they furnish virtually the same curricular material, are less emphatic about their intention or their capacity to undertake the care of the moral and spiritual well-being of their student body.

The present fact is that the Christian colleges have about run out this string. It is difficult enough to compete with schools supported by public authority in terms of salaries and equipment, especially with the contemporary emphasis on scientific research and technology which involves apparatus of horrific cost: but the fact also is that every major institution of higher learning is applying itself to the problem of general education and the nurture of the whole man, and is even making increasing room for "religion" in the process.

These are some of the factors which have generated an increasingly energetic self-scrutiny on the part of the Christian colleges, as exemplified by the two major convocations at Denison, 1954, and at Drake, 1958.

Faith and Learning Under a Common Roof

What follows, then, is addressed to Christian colleges, and by Christian colleges we mean those colleges which have a church connection that still has some meaning to it, in that they are not willing to renounce it. It may be substantial or it may be tenuous: but the decision to cherish it, strengthen it, or renounce it needs to be made in the setting of a theology of the matter as careful as we can make it.

We may begin by examining one or two of what might be called the "standard" justifications of Christian colleges as these are regularly used:

1. We have referred already to the almost monotonous reiteration of the phrase "moral and spiritual values" or phrases very like it.

It is some sign of the distance we have moved away from a thoroughly biblical standpoint when phrases like this gain currency. In their abstraction and lack of definition they are a world removed from biblical language. Actually there is no word in the Bible which could legitimately be translated either *moral* or *values*, and this is not accidental. *Spiritual* does appear, but ordinarily in a sense which is opposite to *sinful*, not opposite to *material*, as our common usage is. The Bible abhors abstraction; it speaks of specific loyalties to a God historically known—not of values or even of principles lacking any definition. The trouble with empty words of this kind is that they take on content from the dominant spirit of the time: and when they become the stock in trade of Christian institutions they leave those institutions horribly vulnerable to infection from without. If our Christian institutions of higher learning are to take the shock of the next period of social and educational history they will have to stand on stronger ground than this.

2. Some representatives of Christian colleges at the Drake Convocation accepted the following statement of their position:

> [they] tend to think of the church colleges as created by the church and existing for its ends (in this connection they use phrases like "the arm of the church"). The colleges are, as it were, established within the church and function as instruments for Christian nurture. Inquiry is "free'" but is to be conducted under Christian direction, so that the truths of reason are always related to the truth as it is in Jesus. The logic of [this position] calls for a faculty committed to the Christian faith, an arrangement which would be regarded by [others] as inimical to a full academic experience.[2]

It is clear that under such a conception the dialectic between faith and culture, and between the community of faith and the community of free inquiry, is inhibited and restricted in order that the church's own ends may be served. The blunt effect is that the educational process is weighted in the Christian interest, and we have seen reason to believe, on the basis of centuries-long experience, that this is in the end to the disadvantage of both faith and culture.

3. Sometimes the church colleges tend to justify themselves on rather matter-of-fact grounds, which yet may have their own importance.

They point to the danger that an educational process conducted under the aegis of public authorities either state or municipal may tend to be monolithic: that it will be streamlined not only to take care of vast numbers of students, but to conform to the popular understanding of what the ends of education are, an understanding which may fall far short of the ideal. They

[2] From a report on "The Church and the Campus," a special issue of *The Christian Scholar* on the Drake University Convocation.

therefore argue that any schools which represent a break in the monolithic structure are to the good, and that it is therefore vital to preserve the existence of small schools which fall outside the (hypothetically) increasingly standardized pattern.

This position gains strength when those who adopt it go on to point out that in institutions vulnerable to public pressure there may be a sad distortion of the curriculum, exemplified in the current case by the excessive interest in and emphasis upon scientific disciplines: so that independent and specifically church colleges have the function of keeping liberal learning alive in all its range and balance.

There is substance in all this, but it is clear that the argument operates not so much as a justification of church colleges specifically as such, but of every independent college of whatever character, religious or other.

4. Whatever provisional strength these arguments may or may not have separately or together, it seems to me clear that they do not rest upon sufficiently solid theological ground. They are governed neither by a strongly wrought theology of culture and of the intellectual life, nor by any real rationale of the relation between the Community of Faith and the Community of Culture as it might be developed out of the long tradition.

There was a second position articulated at Drake University which seems to have more hope in it. The report of the Convocation records it as follows:

> The Community of Faith and the Community of Learning [are] two given orders of life ordained by God for specific functions (just as is the state in its own role) and therefore having their own inherent obligations and their own inherent logic of life. In the Western tradition they are always related but never completely conjoined, and their separateness is the condition of their service each to the other. They exist in creative tension, serving in the one case faith, in the other reason. They are obligated to be fair each to the other in terms of their common obligation to the one Lord. By the accident of American history or by the providence of God, these two orders of life are brought into a relation of peculiar intimacy in the so-called church-related college; but the fact that they live on the same ground does not obliterate their separate roles; they are still obligated to be totally fair each to the other and to honor their respective and distinctive functions. From this point of view the church owes to the college the conditions of its full existence, specifically total freedom of inquiry even where such inquiry offers a *prima facie* threat to the church's cherished conviction and even to the faith of its members.[3]

We can set out our own positive statement of the Vocation of the Christian College by way of a commentary on this, as I see it, sound and true statement.

This means, that when the church for whatever reasons, historical or other, accepts responsibility for some part of the work of higher education, its first obligation is to the work itself. Just as, in the analogous area of political power, the concern of the church should be for political justice and not for a state at the service of the church (this latter breeds the objectionable phenomena of "political Protestantism," "political Catholicism"), so here: the church loses all right to

[3] *Ibid.*

hold the work of higher education under its aegis if it does any violence to the conditions to true education for any reason whatever, even a "Christian" reason. It owes to the Community of Learning, now closely dependent upon the church, the conditions for its full and free functioning, and that without reduction, restriction, or restraint. Specifically it means, for the very health of the work of learning, that it must be conducted under conditions of totally free inquiry, let the chips fall where they may. The church should in fact not only match the independent liberal university in constant vigilance at this point, but should be prepared to use whatever strength and authority it has to ward off the kind of pressures to which the liberal university is always subject, from public opinion, from partisan benefactors, and from within the church itself.

The Commission of the Convocation is right to insist that at this point the church must accept *for* itself whatever hazards are involved *to* itself: for free inquiry may veer away from Christian ground and may call in question not only the church's established convictions, but the "faith" of its members. Yet if the church will not accept whatever risks are here involved it should not pretend to be presiding over the work of higher education: for by the very process of constriction it does violence to the work for which it has accepted responsibility.

If this point is accepted the implications are considerable, and some of them I confess I do not see with any clarity. What does it mean, for example, for the selection of faculty? It would appear to require the end of dogmatic tests for faculty members, on the ground that the intellectual discussion should be fertilized by a variety of points of view, not all of them pious. It is not sufficient to enjoin believing faculty to do justice to unbelieving points of view, since one of the insights which would derive from the wholesome doctrine of Original Sin would be that not even the Christians can be trusted to do justice to points of view antithetical to their own. Yet it becomes a bit invidious if a faculty member is hired explicitly because of his unbelief, to be a kind of professional atheist on the Christian campus! It seems clear that in a situation which is inherently difficult, the church must secure its enlightened "control" over the ongoing purposes of the institution by retaining certain key positions in the hands of believing men—but I cannot be too thankful that I am not an administrator responsible for deciding what these positions are. It seems equally clear, though, that the general run of faculty appointments should be made purely on scholarly merit, with due regard to wholesome variety of conviction, but without any striving after an engineered orthodoxy.

In the second place, though, the church may rightly use its prerogatives to make certain, with every regard to scholarly decency and fairness, that the Christian case is made, that the heritage of Christian theology is available for scrutiny, and that in its full-blooded form. This has the most varied implications for what goes on in the college church or chapel, where the liturgical life of the church should have its fullest and most worthy expression. It means an undergraduate program in Christian theology, taught presumably not in a separate department, but in relation to the various disciplines. Whatever is done should be done not in order that the Community of Faith should swallow up the Community of Learning, but in order that they should be in full and free conversation with each other.

If the Christian college somewhat after this fashion is able to conduct a continual experiment in the fruitful relation of faith and learning, it may well be that it can fill a crucial role for the whole work of higher education: it will become a breeding ground for men and women in whose minds and hearts these issues are alive and real, but who, moreover, have a clue or two to the way in which they ought to be worked out. As such men and women fan out through the whole territory of higher education they may well bring to it new illumination on the problems that so sorely vex it, and they will do so with a devotion to faith and to learning which teaches them that if the two are to be wholesomely conjoined they must be properly distinguished each from the other.

But if this position is to be made good some further things have to be noticed:

1. It is not possible to conduct a fruitful experiment in the relation of Faith and Education unless the education be of first-rate quality. At any lower level no useful lessons will be learned.

This points to some wholesome economy of effort on the part of the churches as they assess the responsibility they can and ought to bear in this whole matter. If they struggle to sustain schools of secondary quality it means that they must fall back for justification on one or other of the arguments for their existence which we saw reason to question. If, on the other hand, they will put their limited resources into schools of high degree, they may make those schools points of light and health, and find for themselves a role in higher education which is not only strategic but indispensable. Of course I am for the moment avoiding all the problems of politics and interest which inhibit free decision in matters as touchy as this: but we shall get nowhere if we do not know what we are after, and what we are after can be defined only out of a Protestant theology of higher education which has been sadly obscured and which sorely needs to be recovered.

2. There can be no illusion about the fact that a dedication to this kind of work in our Christian colleges will require an arduous and sustained "selling job" among the supporters of the schools.

In the first place, we can give no easy assurances about the effect of participation in the life of the colleges upon the minds of their young people. We probably do deal with a good many people whose concern is not so much that their sons' and daughters' minds be matured as that their morals be monitored. Whereas all the assurance we can give them, if the case now being argued be accepted, is that they will be thrown into the rough and tumble of intellectual debate, that all the alternatives will be canvassed, and that all we can promise is that the students will hear the Christian case, as far as we can accomplish this, at its full-blooded best. Even this may be poor comfort, however; because to hear the Christian case at its full-blooded best means to be exposed to the Christian challenge at its most onerous and demanding, and there can be no assurance that this may not set Junior off on the most costly and dangerous adventuring, far beyond the compass of parental planning. But we would be less than honest if we did not acknowledge that we have nothing less in store for those who are exposed to our Christian and scholarly ministrations.

In more general terms, we have to win our constituency to support of an academic undertaking which is not guaranteed to produce "Christian" results in any narrow sense, but is designed rather to honor God with the best service of our minds, and to put the Christian case to the godly hazard of free discussion. What the prospect of such an appeal would be I have no faintest conception; it would depend, I would suppose, upon the energy and insight with which it were pressed. But I have a hopeful conviction that although there are risks to this undertaking which might chill the blood of the hardiest administrator, it is justified not only by the merits of the cause itself, but on the basis that it might well win the support not only of the more narrowly pious, but of many who care for sound learning and would be glad to stand behind a church which was manifestly seeking sound contemporary expression for its age-old devotion to the same good cause.

* * *

If the writer may be permitted a more intimately personal word in relation to this present chapter: it is that I have had the sense in writing it not only that the issues in themselves are delicate and difficult, but also that I talk about them with small authority. Not only are these problems peculiarly American, and American history is not my history, but I have such acquaintance with them as I do have only by reason of a somewhat intensive but very brief participation in discussion about them.

Nonetheless they are part of the general issue which I am commissioned to deal with: and I must simply submit these provisional reflections to the judgment of those who know the problem more intimately, and who are more immediately responsible for its solution. I really don't care what rough handling the present argument may take, if it contributes to the discussion now going forward, a discussion which by the grace of God may give us a Protestant theology not only adequate to illuminate the problems of the Christian colleges, but to sustain and enliven the work of higher education wherever it is done.

CHAPTER EIGHT

GOOD CITIZENSHIP IN THE COMMONWEALTH OF LEARNING

As we turn now to consider the concrete form of Christian obligation in the academic community, we are bound to reflect, a little shamefacedly, that over the recent period the church has been prone to consider the university either as a threat to its cherished convictions, or as a field for missionary endeavor, rather than as an area of positive Christian responsibility. But if the main thrust of the argument so far is in the right direction, then we are bound to take the academic community to be in some sense "ordained of God" for purposes of his own and therefore of its own: so that as with the state so with the university, the first form of Christian responsibility is to sustain the order which God has appointed, and to help it do its work well; for, as we heard from Newman, "What the empire is in political history, such is the university in the sphere of philosophy and research."

Actually the main expression of Christian cultural concern over recent generations has been in relation to political justice: this is an area in which on the whole we are at home, and in which we have accumulated resources out of the long tradition for the handling of the contemporary political issue. I propose therefore to take the *triad* (*sacerdotium, imperium, studium*) seriously, and to see what we can arrive at if we treat the academic community on the analogy of the political community.

The Analogy of the Political Community

There are certain affirmations about the state which are part and parcel of the continuing tradition of Christian thought in its central expression, and especially in its Protestant expression:

1. *It is ordained of God.* The phrase itself of course originates with Paul (Romans 13), and it may be readily agreed that the interpretation of it has changed with changing political circumstances. During the long centuries when single sovereignty was the characteristic form of political power, with no viable alternative in sight, it was used by Christian commentators to lend sanction to the power of the monarch, while it reminded him that he was responsible to God for the order over which he presided. When in the transition from medievalism to the modern world of independent nations the national sovereigns slipped the reins of church authority and it became necessary to develop constitutional safeguards against royal abuse, and to vindicate eventually the right of revolution, then the exegesis shifted to the context of the phrase. Puritan commentators took pains to remind the sovereign that he was ordained of God "for good"—or, as I Peter had put it, "for the punishment of evildoers and the praise of them that do well." The implication was that if the

king busied himself with the praise of evildoers and the punishment of them that did well—if, that is, he played favorites against the general interest, or allowed intolerable injustice to hide behind the royal robes—then in terms of God's veritable ordinance he might be restrained, or replaced by a monarch who knew better and performed better the work for which he was "ordained."

These fluctuations of interpretation are undeniable, and the tracing of them of considerable fascination; but behind them all there is the consistent conviction that political order is in the purpose of God, that the governance of states is a godly activity to which a man may apply himself with a good conscience, and that Christian men especially should sense the peculiar urgency of the work in terms of God's known will and the common good, and should apply themselves to it with particular diligence.

As with the empire, then, so with the university: as the political order is ordained of God for justice, so the Commonwealth of Learning is ordained of God for the wholesome pursuit of knowledge. As the state after the old formula is "the secular arm" (of God, not of the church, as we shall see) so the university as the chief custodian of the enterprise of learning serves God well when it does well its proper work. The state ought not to be diverted from the work of justice to serve either a lower or a higher end; manifestly it ought not to become the instrument of injustice, but less obviously, though not less truly, it should not be diverted from the plain work of justice to save souls or to try to bring the kingdom of God about. For these ends it is neither appointed nor is it fitted. So with the university: its proper work is the work of scholarship, and it ought not to be diverted from it; manifestly it ought not to serve untruth, but less obviously, yet not less truly, it ought not to serve piety. For this latter it is neither appointed nor fitted.

2. *It does not exist to serve the church, but to serve justice.* The last point can be made more explicit, again in terms of the political tradition.

Large tracts of Christian reflection on the state were bedeviled by the notion that since the end of all human activity is the salvation of the soul, the state must be subordinated to this end. The origins of this notion are complex and cannot here be analyzed, but the effect of it is clear. It meant in practice that since the state is itself manifestly not organized or equipped to get men to heaven, it best contributes to this end by putting itself at the service of the church. The test of states therefore tended to be their cordiality to the church institution, rather than their service of general justice. Protestants still point with some scorn to the tendency of the Roman Catholic hierarchy to favor those governments which are more conspicuous for their ecclesiastical piety than for their service of the common human good: but there is a corresponding form of "political Protestantism" which tends to assess the merits of aspirants for political office less by their capacity to handle the practicalities of power and interest than by their overt piety and their regularity in church. These pious criteria are not only dubious in themselves—since no amount of piety guarantees political prudence; but they are hard to apply—since piety can easily be counterfeited. "Paris is worth a Mass," as Henry of Navarre put it succinctly.

But the error here lies deeper, and in this area as in so many other the Reformation effected an important clarification. By the recovered insight that salvation is not a human achievement (still less an ecclesiastical or political achievement) but the gift of God, the Reformation freed both church and state from an anxious concern with matters beyond their competence, and directed them to the work for which they were severally appointed: the Gospel witness in the case of the church, the work of justice in the case of the state. The state in particular was to be tested, not by its service to the ecclesiastical institution, but by its service of general justice. This is in line with earlier insights, which as we saw made the state not only responsible for general justice, but made it responsible for reminding the church that the interests of general justice might have little to do with the interests of the ecclesiastical institution.

So, by analogy, the university. It must resist every attempt, however well or piously intended, to suborn it from its own proper function, which is to serve truth and not to serve salvation, still less to serve the ecclesiastical interest. Men are saved no more by knowledge than by power, and so the mechanisms of power and of learning need not be manipulated in the interest of salvation. The doctrine of justification by faith—the recognition that salvation is mediated in love and not secured by any kind of wisdom—is in this area a charter of emancipation for the life of the mind and for those institutions dedicated to it: for, if we are not saved by being right in intellectual matters, then we need not fear to be wrong and may go about our work of inquiry garrisoned by the conviction which is born of the Gospel, that we are not going to thrust beyond the reach of the inexorable love of God by following the facts where they lead.

The university, then, exists to serve truth and not to serve the church; but this has further implications.

3. *The best government is not the most pious.* This has been suggested already, but the Reformation Confessions are explicit about it: that the "magistrate," that is to say, the political officer, is neither qualified for his office by piety nor disqualified for it by impiety. The Confessions are explicit, though it would be difficult to claim that the communities of the Reformation accepted the implications of the doctrine with entire consistency. They do not do so, as we have seen, even now. And yet what is here affirmed is clearly implied in the renunciation of the "sacral state" with its subordination of state to church. For if the state is established in the interest of justice in independence of the church, then ecclesiastical tests are out, and state officials are to be tested not by their piety but by their

understanding of what justice means and their capacity to secure it. They are to be tested not by their formal acknowledgment of God but by their attention to the work he has given them to do.

Here the analogy, in the case of the university, is very clear; and we shall have occasion to return to it. Shortly put, it means that the condition for admission to and leadership in the Commonwealth of Learning is not piety but scholarly competence. It means that we can understand what the tradition meant when it spoke of academic workers as *milites Christi,* and it means that Christian citizens of the Commonwealth of Learning can hail the unbelieving scholar as a comrade-in-arms, fighting with him the Holy War on the front of scholarship, even if the devoted infidel does not know whose service he is in.

4. *The Christian contributes both service and criticism.* The state is, in the New Testament sense of the term, one of the "powers" of this world. It is subordinate to God, and has its own legitimacy within its proper sphere; but like all the subordinate powers it is tempted by the sin with which it is infected to "exalt itself" against God. In the case of the state the forms of abuse to which it is subject are all too well known: it is tempted to make excessive claims for itself; it is liable to be seduced from the service of God, which is the work of justice, to the service of those interests which are most powerful and which can offer the largest bribes.

So while the Christian who knows something of the mechanisms of God's government of the world will be eager to sustain the state in the performance of its proper work, he will be alert also to rebuke and restrain it when it falsifies its office or when it claims prerogatives that do not belong to it. But of this legitimate and necessary criticism there are two things to be said: in the first place, the state is to be criticized in terms of its own proper function, not in terms of some specifically Christian interest; and, in the second place, the efficacy of the Christian's criticism will be in precise proportion to the diligence and thoroughness with which he performs the positive work of citizenship.

So again with the university. The Christian citizen of the Commonwealth of Learning has the function both of sustaining it and of criticizing it: but his criticism will be born of jealous concern that the university live up to its calling; and its effectiveness will be proportionate to the Christian's own devotion and trained application to the ends for which the university is established.

The Christian citizen of the Commonwealth of Learning, then, is committed to disinterested service of that community which is at least the chief citadel of cultural concern: his business within it is not in the first instance to grind a Christian axe, but to help the scholarly institution to be true to itself and to its calling.

What this more specifically involves we may see

more clearly if we consider the separate roles that Christians play.[1]

The Teacher

It follows from all that has been said thus far that the initial responsibility of the Christian teacher is the cultivation and the exercise of those qualities on which the effectual life of the Commonwealth of Learning depends. At this level he is one citizen among others, and the tasks that fall to him are those that fall to any member of the Commonwealth. In specific they are the following:

1. The full and faithful performance of his "profession." Even the term *professor* will have a peculiarly vivid meaning for him, by analogy with the life of faith, in which to *profess* is to *confess* or to declare without fear or favor the truth by which he is held. But this added dimension of devotion will not alter the *form* of his activity: it will mean only that he will bring to the work of scholarship and teaching an added diligence and an added depth. For him any kind of slovenliness either in research or communication will be not only a professional lapse in the ordinary sense, but a kind of blasphemy. He will cultivate those peculiar

[1] Since the book must end sometime, I am omitting any specific treatment of the work of the administrator, the public relations man, or for that matter the football coach. Whatever be the true conception of their various roles, let it be agreed, as I think it would be without difficulty, that their roles are auxiliary to the work of scholarship and teaching, and have to be understood in relation to it.

virtues which are not a monopoly of the Christians but the glory of the intellectual community. As Von Hügel puts it,

> The intellectual virtues are no mere empty name: candor, moral courage, intellectual honesty, scrupulous accuracy, chivalrous fairness, endless docility to facts, disinterested collaboration, unconquerable hopefulness, perseverance, manly renunciation of popularity and easy honors, love of bracing labor and strengthening solitude, these and many other cognate qualities bear upon them the impress of God and of his Christ.[2]

Some of these may seem at first sight not to be intellectual virtues in the strict sense at all: *courage,* for example. But surely it is clear on the basis of common observation or even of rigorous self-examination that cowardice is a worse enemy of true wisdom than is ignorance, even when that ignorance is culpable; for while ignorance merely obscures knowledge, cowardice perverts it.

Upon the full and faithful performance of this primary obligation all else depends; in this matter the righteousness of the Christian academic man must exceed that of the Scribes and Pharisees—which is to say, those whose activity is generated from sources and from motives other than the Christian. It is at this point that he stands or falls: for no other service which he may wish to bring to the university—for example, the wholesome work of criticism—can be of the slightest effect if he fails here.

[2] *The Mystical Element of Religion,* Vol. I, p. 79, quoted by Coleman, *The Task of the Christian in the University* (New York: Association Press, 1947), pp. 58-59.

He will bring also to the performance of his scholarly office a clear vision of its meaning, a vision which will not change the character of the office but will hold it from distortion and lend it its proper dignity: his relation, for example, to his subject matter, on the one hand, and to his students, on the other. Toward the former he brings a reverence and a delicacy born of the apprehension that the heritage of learning is a gift of God, and that as in the historical arena God has had strange "Messiahs," so in the realm of scholarship the ongoing work of learning owes much to the infidels—for example, to Voltaire and to Nietzsche. Toward the latter, the students, his concern is not only the care of the conscientious craftsman that his apprentices should be thoroughly furnished unto every good scholarly work, but the recognition that a common activity in learning generates relationships of confidence which can be both fruitful and burdensome, but must be taken seriously. Says Jacques Barzun:

> The teacher hears it all—the quarrels with contemporaries, the disappointments and injustices in campus affairs, the girls that charm but leave insatiate, and most persistently, the vision of the good life clearly seen but lying inaccessible on a pathless height.[3]

His role will be that of a faithful midwife, whose service of a creative process which he did not initiate and whose issue is beyond his mastery depends upon a

[3] *Teacher in America* (New York: Anchor Books, 1954), p. 197.

reverence and care in handling both the subject matter and the human matter.

2. His right to citizenship established, the Christian teacher will serve the commonwealth in ways characteristic of every *polis:* by defending it against disorder from within and against attack from without. He will be in the hottest part of the battle against tyranny or anarchy, seeking with constant diligence the freedom and balance which belong to the authentic life of the commonwealth. He will be ever on guard against pressures from without which might threaten the integrity of the university, or seduce it from its proper work. And he will be peculiarly wary, partly because he knows the danger so well, of pressures emanating from the church itself, which is congenitally tempted to see in free inquiry a threat to saving orthodoxy. Here again he will find resource in the "orthodox" Newman, who insists that intellectual work can not be well done if the scholar is constantly compelled to look over his shoulder at the theologian: ". . . if we invite reason to take its place in our schools, we must let reason have fair and full play. If we reason, we must submit to the conditions of reason. We cannot use it by halves. . . ." And in this internal and external defense of the university he will attend, in Blake's phrase, to "the minute particulars," to the sordid details of tenure and the proper use of the tax power, and will have to find that difficult balance between cultural work and committee work, for which the only solution is service to both beyond the call of duty.

3. He will learn to rejoice in "the uncovenanted mercies of God" which are visibly part of academic life: in the first place, the powerful service of God which is done by those who do not acknowledge Him.

> If we believe that the spirit of God is the only fountain of truth, we shall neither reject nor despise the truth wherever it shall appear unless we wish to insult the spirit of God. . . . Shall we esteem anything laudable and excellent which we do not recognize as proceeding from God?[4]

And the same John Calvin:

> They are superstitious who dare not borrow anything from profane writers. For since all truth is from God, if anything has been aptly or truly said by those who have not piety, it ought not to be repudiated, for it came from God. Since then all things are of God, why is it not right to refer to his glory whatever can properly be applied to that?[5]

And if this recognition that they served God after their fashion be allowed to "profane writers" out of the long tradition, it ought not to be withheld from our contemporaries, though we might do well to be a shade tactful about expressing it, since nothing irritates the impious like the allegation of piety! But we may allow ourselves a small share of wry satisfaction not only that the good Lord knows them that are his in the world of scholarship as elsewhere, but that here as elsewhere he makes the wrath of men to turn to his praise: for we have to acknowledge, not reluctantly, that a great amount of scholarly work of high quality is generated

[4] John Calvin, *Institutes,* Book II, ch. ii, para. 15.
[5] *Commentary on Titus,* Opera III.

by professional jealousy, sinful emulation, and the lust for power and status.

The Calvinists among us in particular should have no difficulty in acknowledging that there may be a real sense in which God "elects" atheists to fill an indispensable role as the scourge of the Christians. This does not mean that we should not try to convert them; but the fact that we so seldom succeed may not be without meaning, since nothing could be more inimical to the vital life of scholarship than a campus monotonously Christian.

4. However, these last paragraphs suggest a further contribution that Christians specifically may bring to the campus when they know their proper business there.

They ought to be able to identify with unusual precision the sins to which the academic flesh is heir; they know them, not to put too fine a point on it, because they know their own academic hearts, and the sins that do so easily beset *them*. The three sins are these:

Cowardice. This, as we have seen, does more than prevent wisdom: it perverts it.

Imperialism. It is a form of idolatry as deadly as any other idolatry. It consists in the attempted aggrandizement of disciplines and departments in whose prestige the prestige of the individual academician is at stake.

Pedantry. This is the most insidious form that pride takes. I shall give first two general descriptions of it, the first from the long-neglected English theologian P. T. Forsyth:

So often . . . you find the finest critical faculty, and the most powerful scholarly apparatus, conjoined with a moral nature singularly naïve, and beautifully simple and unequal to the real world. Their experience of life and conscience has no record of lapse or shame. Their world is a study of still-life; it has not the drama, the fury, the pang, the tragedy, the crisis of the actual world at large, with its horrible guilt and its terror of judgment. . . . They inhabit, morally, the West End.[6]

And from the invaluable Newman:

There are men who embrace in their minds a vast multitude of ideas, but with little sensibility about their real relations towards each other. These may be antiquarians, annalists, naturalists; they may be learned in the law; they may be versed in statistics that are most useful in their own place; I should shrink from speaking disrespectfully of them; still there is nothing in such attainments to guarantee the absence of narrowness of mind. If they are nothing more than well-read men, or men of information, they have not what specially deserves the name of culture of mind, or fulfils the type of liberal education.[7]

But the condition of the pedant is even worse than this. In his wizened growth he is the man who, through no fault of his own, is equipped with nothing but brains. And with his brains he builds his own Tower of Babel in the form of a scholarly specialty, to which indeed he contributes notably but which he comes in time to consider his own private preserve. He resents the intrusion upon it of younger scholars, and resents particularly the disturbance by new conclusions of the "system" on which his prestige rests. His condition in the end is pitiable.

[6] *The Person and Place of Jesus Christ* (London: Independent Press Ltd., 1948), p. 201.

[7] John Henry Newman, *op. cit.*

To all these sins the academic flesh is heir, as the Christian ought to know by the illumination of the Gospel upon the deep and dark places of his own life. He knows also where these ills are to be healed, by the salutary serum of grace which is mediated in the ordinances and fellowship of the committed people of God. These he will seek out for himself: but because he knows also that the scholarly virtues need grace for their sustenance, and the scholarly vices need grace for their correction, he will concern himself, not that the university should become a church which it ought not, but that *in* the university the church be visibly and vitally living out its own authentic existence.

For while much good work gets done for dubious motives and by the grace of Heaven, the more that grace has free course the better in the end of the day the work will be. David Riesman has the right of it:

> . . . an enormous amount of work goes on, which often leads to new findings, simply to prove that some other professor is wrong or crazy or has missed something. Freedom of speech or of investigation would, I fear, soon die out if they could be claimed only by the pure in heart, though I also fear that in many important areas they are dying because we lack the saving remnant of a few who *are* pure in heart.[8]

The Student

In these degenerate days of pupil-centered education, a notion that tends to carry over into the college and university, it is well to insist in the first place that there

[8] *Constraint and Variety in American Education* (Lincoln, Neb.: University of Nebraska Press, 1956). Used by permission.

can be a university *without* students. Indeed there *have* been universities without students: for example, during the war years in Britain the stream of admissions to the universities dried up, in some cases completely. But this did not mean that the institution folded: the Guild of Scholars simply got on with its scholarly work, for the time being without any apprentices. Of course, for the continuance of its life the Guild of Scholars (one ancient name for what we now call the faculty) needs apprentices: but this ancient relation between craftsman and apprentice is worth recalling, if only to get things in proportion. The university cannot get along without faculty, though it might contrive to get along for a time simply by using the resources of that "congealed faculty" which is the university library. All of this actually is only half-serious: the fact is that the university exists, certainly not for the sake of the students, nor even for the sake of the faculty: it exists for the sake of something "bigger than both of them," that heritage of humane and scientific learning which it is commissioned to appropriate, improve, and transmit.

But the old notion that the student is an apprentice in the Guild of Scholars is enough to call in question many of the attitudes and ambitions by which the student mind tends to be infected. It means that admission to the Guild of Scholars, even at the apprentice level, is on condition; and the condition is not simply the payment of fees (though that contribution to the expenses of the institution helps to feed, clothe, house, and equip the senior craftsmen) but a readiness for the wholesome disciplines of the craft, which as we have seen are onerous and exacting. The notion is much too widely held that for the payment of that somewhat meager proportion of the cost of the enterprise which the student pays, he in effect "buys" an education, and it is thereafter the responsibility of the university to supply it. I notice, for example, that far too often, when a student for the best of reasons is given a poor or a failing grade, his reaction is to search through every possible option for an explanation of this intolerable situation: the teacher has a grudge against him, or the examination is poorly drawn, or he (or she) was in bad psychological shape to take it, or the university has fallen down on its responsibility, or the wrong government is in power in Washington—anything rather than face the fact that he doesn't have the brains for the work, or didn't work hard enough at it, or both.

This somewhat irritable preamble is a rather negative way to come at the work of a student; but it needs saying, and the point needs to be pressed home in a somewhat more positive fashion. There are grand and glorious exceptions, and more of the exceptions ought to be Christian, but for whatever complex reasons (and no doubt the faculty must take some of the blame for it), I think it is true that the present temper of our student bodies lacks two qualities which have distinguished the Community of Learning when it has been at its best: I mean *rigor* and *exuberance*. And these two belong together when it is scholarly work which is in question: for the adventure of learning not only is a matter of high excitement, but it demands for its performance, along with a certain exhilaration in the enterprise, a most notable rigor if it is to be well performed. Instead we have a rather pervasive flaccidity which affects not only the immediate work of learning, but all that students do. They are so preoccupied with themselves, and with the diverse ways in which the university enterprise may fatten their prestige or their prospects, that the tide of intellectual eagerness seldom catches and carries them. Even their off-time occupations are affected: for there is all the difference in the world between the dreary naughtiness which is dismally contrived as an excuse for not working, and the hearty blowing-off-steam which is almost necessitated as a relief from working to the point of strain. Society has always been tolerant of student high spirits which were the concomitant of an exhausting scholarly grind: but it has and need have small patience with adolescent naughtiness which simply advertises an incapacity to do any good work at all.

The sign, of course, that we are indeed engaged on an enterprise that is bigger than we are is that occasionally the sheer excitement of the thing breaks through. The characteristic situation is that of the student seminar: where during the first session or two the tendency is for the whole undertaking to be vitiated by the preoccupation of the members with the figure they are cutting rather than with the material they are studying. They make the carefully calculated comment: daring enough to help them catch the professor's eye, but not so daring as to mark them as an "odd ball." The whole enterprise begins to become rewarding when there takes place, as does take place on occasions, something almost analogous to a religious conversion: when the preoccupation of each self with itself and its self-image is swallowed up in the demanding claims of the truth itself, and the discussion moves from self-conscious posturing to an absorbed and unself-conscious preoccupation with wresting from the material whatever truth it has.

And this brings us close to the first thing that ought to be said about the Christian student.

HIS STUDIES

The emancipating effect of the Gospel ought to be that the Christian student is the first to be freed from crippling self-preoccupation to accept with exuberance the rigors of the scholarly task, done not to minister to the self's self-esteem, but to honor God with the best service of the mind. In the intellectual warfare the Christians ought to be not only *milites Christi* fighting alongside every other slogging foot soldier, but they ought to be the shock troops who are prepared to press every inquiry further than others might dare to take it, fearing no truth, content with no half-truth, never claiming to know all truth. It may be almost too much to affirm that as they enter the library they should hear the sound of distant trumpets; yet I suppose that nothing less than this was intended by the ancient insistence that a scholar at his proper work is a soldier in the service of Christ.

Without getting into details of study skills and the like, it may be to the point to identify one or two of the things that tend to obscure the high meaning and to prevent the full fruitfulness of the work of study.

In the first place, it has to be recognized that the facts of undergraduate life suggest that much of what I have written is romantic in the last degree: that the entering student for one thing is simply not equipped to undertake scholarly work at such a demanding level, or to do more than grub and dig for the minimum information that will keep him academically solvent. It must be for some such reason as this that I find students who talk of "academic" and "intellectual" life, which ought to be synonymous, as if they were antithetical, the notion being that *academic* demands are so heavy that there is no time for *intellectual* activity. Data pile up in notebooks, but they never yield up their meaning in such fashion that the student would sense the excitement of discovering connections, seeing light on dark places, or penetrating at least some way into the mystery of life and history. It reminds me of the story of the traveler to a Southern town who stepped off the train (the town was new to him) and asked the porter for directions. Said the porter, "You know the Post Office?" "No, I'm afraid not." "You know the Town Hall?" "No, I'm sorry." "The Police Station?" "No." "Boss," said the porter, "you ain't got enough information to *take* instruction." And when I have the student in my office who is baffled to be told he's missed the point when he had really no idea there *was* a point, I have to bite my tongue to stop the comment: "Boss, you ain't got enough information to *take* instruction."

The fact is that by reason of the manifold distractions or the sheer tiredness of our present social order or the poverty of our high school work—who knows?—but whatever the reason, many of the present student generation are so far behind with decent general reading that they have no matrix of beginning culture into which to fit new facts. The Christian who knows himself yoked in Christ to the whole body of humanity will be eager, and that right early, to make his own as much of the human story as he can read, mark, and digest; and the more of it he can absorb the more able he will be with decent economy of effort to identify the new fact and "place" it in his developing picture of the world.

There is another factor which makes for a certain contemporary indecisiveness and flaccidity in intellectual work. From somewhere or other has come the notion that anything in the shape of a *conviction* is faintly disreputable. It is not only the absence of a frame of reference that makes it difficult to "place" the new fact and render a verdict on it, but the sense that all facts float in such a mist of relativity that it is slightly risky even to admit you see them, since some legerdemain of scholarship may shortly snatch them away from you, so that what was fact will be fact no longer. A decent tentativeness is a wholesome expression of a proper human and scholarly humility; but we seem to have rather a sort of *dogmatic* tentativeness which suggests that it is intellectually indecent to make up your mind. The open mind is good, but as G. K. Chesterton said in this connection, the point of an open mouth is to close it on something—and so with the open mind. To snap the mind shut on the facts as you see them is not the end of inquiry: for if you never form convictions how are you going to test them? The present situation tends to be that the university whose proper business is to test and try convictions by rubbing them against one another in the healthy friction of free debate, is hard put to it to find men of conviction firm enough to stand up and be tested. I am not for a moment suggesting that we should pretend a conviction we do not feel; but I *am* suggesting that we can let the facts as we see them have their way with us, and not feel bound to avoid a judgment on them as if *that* were a matter of principle. I think it is Moberly who says that there is no more merit to the empty mind than to the closed mind: we ought to abjure both.

HIS RELIGION

In the measure in which the student comes under the influence of authentic Christian conviction he ought to be on the way to full and uncoerced and unself-conscious application to the work of learning; he will see the human heritage and the material of scholarship as the gift of God and the raw material for his scholarly work; he will be eager to drive beyond the data to the "story," since the whole human and historic tale is the family history of those who are his kin in Christ; and he will be learning the secret of that wholesome mixture of conviction and humility which is prepared to follow what light it sees as a condition of having more light, which will not claim more for his truth than that it *is* his truth, but that since it *is* his truth he is content to live by it until new truth enforces its revision.

The unhappy fact is that current-style piety does not always work that way.

The marks of characteristic student piety are relatively easy to identify, and would be agreed upon, I think, by most of those who have to live with it.

In the first place, it is too *amorphous* to provide a strong undergirding for scholarly work or for anything else. It tends to reject the Christian frame of doctrine and of discipline for an undefined "belief" in an undifferentiated "godness" which is little better than an oblong blur in the mind. Dogma is suspect because it is conceived to be constricting, but the unfocused piety that takes its place is a testimony rather to American amiability than to any breadth or depth of religious vision.

In the second place, it tends to feed that very *self-preoccupation* which is the enemy of disinterested and unself-conscious application to the work in hand. Instead of freeing the self from itself it fosters concern with the self's maturity (if it is liberal religion) or the self's salvation (if it is conservative); and it even has its own programatic devices for fostering this kind of self-concern. But, as Jacques Barzun says, "Young people think sufficiently about themselves not to make them do it on schedule," and it is not only a pragmatic interest in getting the work of scholarship well and truly done, but a conviction about the character of Christian faith itself, which affirms that it is the nature of that faith to lift the focus off the self and put it on the work in hand, in this case the work of the mind as it serves truth for very love of God.

Worse still, there are too many instances where not only does a vague or inverted piety lend no aid to the work of learning, but where a spurious piety prevents it. Sometimes piety works the very mischief with scholarship. I could recount more than one case where in varying phrases I have been told that "God has spoken; it is no longer necessary to think." But even where the thing is not so brash as that, there is a more subtly destructive relation between piety and learning which seems to work like this: I have seen a student who was spurred to work of decent quality by the ordinary human motives of status, reward, and the like: but when he "got religion" the level of his work fell off quite drastically. He did not (I speak of more than one instance), like one devout young lady, "give up study because it interfered with her work for Christ"; but he took some pious pride that he was rid of the old cravings for status and reward. The effect was work of squalid quality. I think we have here a campus illustration of our Lord's story about the house with seven devils: the hazard of evicting them is that if the house is left swept and garnished it may be taken over by seven devils worse than the first—in the present case, by normal human sloth and indolence.

It is a rare and lovely thing—I suppose an academic instance of what Reinhold Niebuhr would call the "impossible possibility"—that those who are Christ's should do for his sake a work of the mind which excels anything they could have accomplished under the ancient human spurs. Yet that is the possibility to which we are called: that here again our righteousness should exceed that of the Scribes, and that there should well up from the secret depths of the devoted Christian heart a motive for good craftsmanship within the Guild of Scholars more powerful than the goad of ambition, or any other goad whatever. "To think well," said Thomas Traherne, "is to serve God in the interior court." Yet we are not left to our own poor resources at this point; for every Christian group that knows its proper business in the university community should be diligent not only to hold its members to their primary responsibility, but to sustain them in performing it; to permit no programatic distractions from this number one priority, but rather to make the work and worship of the group a strong prop for every scholarly resolve.

HIS PROBLEMS

Since this section began with the reminder that there can be a university without students, it is a shade paradoxical that we have already given inordinate space to their concerns. There remains the whole business of that characteristic range of problems which torment the student, and some of which torment in particular the Christian student; but they would require for their decent treatment another book of at least this length. They range from the present status of the debate between science and religion, to the problems of predestination and the fate of the unconverted heathen, the vexing claim of the Christian faith to a uniqueness and finality over against other "religions," the relativity of all knowledge, and so on till the dormitory lights go out.

No one man can be competent in all of them, and in any event there is no one of them on which sound Christian comment can not be found by those who have the will to look for it. But there is one quite general statement that might perhaps usefully be made, and it has application, I think, to all of them. It is this, in words already quoted from Newman: "It is the highest wisdom to accept truth of whatever kind, wherever it is clearly ascertained to be such, though there be difficulty in adjusting it with other known truth."

In general that is sound and true, but it stops short of speaking to the real distress of mind in which many of us are sometimes caught, when we are tossed into the maelstrom of the university debate, ". . . a meeting-place for every conceivable ideology—where Mom's religion, Dad's politics and Miss Jones' history will have to cross blades with everything from Kropotkin's anarchism to quantum theory and Hegelian dialectic.[9]

[9] Marvin Deckoff in *Life,* March 30, 1953.

What is to happen, to bring the matter to the sharpest point, when new fact and new understanding seem to call in question one's most cherished conviction, specifically one's Christian conviction as far as one knows what it is and the grounds on which it rests? "Have I the right to keep my faith at the price of my intellectual integrity?" as I had it from one troubled student. The provisional answer was "No," that intellectual integrity is *part* of any faith worth the name, certainly of Christian faith.

But something more ought to be said, and since it must be said shortly let me put it this way: that there is no honesty and no hope in simply digging in on a Christian position that seems to be discredited, and some honesty but little more hope in capitulating to the secular alternative. The only really hopeful procedure, when the facts seem to conflict with the faith, is to press investigation further into both facts and faith. It may be that all the facts are not in, and it may be that all the faith is not known. How often I have seen students bereft and stricken at the prospect of having to abandon a faith which actually was due for the trash can: an adolescent, superstitious faith that bore small resemblance to the Christian faith in its full and mature expression.

To be practical about it: it is premature to put the Christian view of man in the discard for a secular alternative before one has mastered, say, Reinhold Niebuhr's *Nature and Destiny of Man* in which every secular alternative is canvassed, and the Christian doctrine strongly reaffirmed. But this is only one instance of a sound working principle. Of course, in the nature of the case there can be no guarantee that a double investigation into the faith and the facts, however far it is pressed, will bring the two together again: but there is no hope in any road except this double road. The charter for it is in the Gospel itself: that no honest inquiry, nor even honest denial of God, will separate us from the God (say, if you like, if there be such a God) who loves truth because he is the source of it, and who in the realm of the mind separates himself only from the hypocrites.

The Beginning of Wisdom

"The fear of the Lord is *the beginning of wisdom.*" This recurrent biblical phrase will serve as a caption for a section which is, frankly, a kind of catch-all for certain points I want to make, which did not go easily into the sequence of the argument thus far. The phrase has a very general relevance and a variety of applications to both faculty and students, and to all who make knowledge their stock in trade.

In the first place, it constitutes a reminder that "a mere scholar is an intelligible ass," a saying which is as true today as when Sir Thomas Overbury coined it in the seventeenth century. Wisdom is not apart from the work of the mind, but it is not inevitably the product of the work of the mind: it is attainable only when the mind is garrisoned by disciplines which preserve it from arrogance and which hold it to its proper work, of which disciplines the chief are *reverence* before the encompassing mystery, the *humility* which knows that our truth is always less true than we think it, and the *compassion* which reminds us constantly that "truth is in order to goodness." All these are the fruit of "the fear of the Lord" in the pregnant sense in which the Bible uses the term, a "fear" which is akin to that love which, as Dostoevsky says, is "a fierce and terrible thing." And this fear that is love is nourished best in the Community of Faith, which is the appointed place of God's meeting with his people, and so makes it vital that the Community of Faith be close joined to the Community of Learning and in constant traffic with it. It was William James, a philosopher himself, who said at the end of a lifetime with scholars that he had at last discovered what philosophers most wanted: it was *praise.* It is this common humanity which is both the condition of the scholar's fruitful working and which also can play the very devil with his conclusions; and both for the full development of his humanity and for its emancipation from imprisoning pride he needs more than the ordinary disciplines of his craft: he needs the wholesome ministries of grace, which are the Word, the Sacraments, and the Company of common folk who gather faithfully around them, there to become the beneficiaries of a wisdom wiser than all the wisdom of the wise.

The phrase "the beginning of wisdom" also has a kind of epigrammatic illumination to throw both on the use and the limits of the university experience.

We know the stock reminder, so frequently incorporated in commencement addresses and baccalaureate sermons, that the four undergraduate years represent not the completion but the initiation of an "education" —the "beginning of wisdom." This is trite but true enough: and its meaning need not be spelled out. But I cringe often at the sound of academic oratory: as if those whom we graduate were knights in shining armor, ready to take the leadership of the future—when we who know them know that beneath the shining regalia of graduation is the same messy, human, potentially magnificent material which has been disappointing its own expectations of itself, and just occasionally surprising itself, since the beginning of time. Some of them, as well they know, have "goofed off" continually and are lucky to have made it; in a place dedicated to books they have missed their chance to learn wisdom from the perennial founts of wisdom; they have avoided every vital decision or postponed it, while shouting raucously to keep their courage up.

For many the summons to present themselves for graduation is not so much a challenge to long-prepared-for and dedicated action, as a threat that their bluff is about to be called. The summons to *leadership*, as that is ordinarily understood, has at this point a hollow and ironic sound, *unless*—and this is vital—it be leadership in the Gospel sense of it: that they should be among men as those who serve. This is a vocation for which they are able and in some sense prepared: not that they should stride at the head of the army of humanity, but that they should take their place with some usefulness in the ranks.

For this the four-year grind is a fruitful apprenticeship: they have enough knowledge of the tradition to know both man's greatness and his wretchedness, to have some measure of their own dignity and of their most terrible weakness. They have enough knowledge of the contemporary world in its interlocking necessities to be able, if they will, to make out of their occupation a true Vocation. They know enough of the complexities of civic and political life to be less vulnerable to "the unseen assassins," the slogans which pervert judgment. They know enough of the heroic heritage to know that there is more satisfaction in keeping company with the great than in keeping up with the Joneses, and may be saved from a shapeless conformism not by pretending an independence they cannot sustain, but by the supporting company of the men of faith and courage.

All this they have, if their four years have not been wasted, and all this is good: but it is not good enough. "The fear of the Lord is the beginning of wisdom" in another sense. They need also, if they knew it, what only the Gospel can provide: a love for men generated not out of our poor compassion or their innate worth, but from the knowledge that they and we are equally beloved of God. They need the wholesome knowledge that we are servants of God and not masters of destiny; that our poor wisdom and our poor strength are perfected by his counsel and his might. Given this, they may have courage enough to fight on the frontiers of truth and justice, frontiers which now run through all the areas of our common life: through the community of scholarship, of technology, of commerce and industry, of government, and even through the suburban street where it may be that the fight against stuffiness and prejudice must chiefly be fought.

Doubly fortunate are those who discover during their four years not only the wealth of the complex human heritage, but where the resources for this ceaseless Holy War are to be found: in the sustaining Grace with which the world is filled, in the "homely ordinances" of Book and Sacrament and common prayer which sustain the church and all who belong in it.

Leadership calls for an odd combination of adaptability and doggedness: an adaptability which ought to be the fruit of knowledge, and a doggedness which is the fruit of faith. It is precisely these which ought to be generated out of an encounter between the Community of Learning and the Community of Faith as they meet in the life and inform the growth of the individual student. This is what would seem to be meant by human and Christian maturity. It joins good citizenship in the Commonwealth of Learning to good citizenship in the wider society, both comprehended in a total life of Faith.

BIBLIOGRAPHY

Basic Books

JOHN HENRY NEWMAN, *The Scope and Nature of University Education,* 1859 (New York: Dutton, Everyman, 1958). Available with additional material as *The Idea of a University,* 1873 (New York: Doubleday, Image, 1959).

ARNOLD S. NASH, *The University in the Modern World* (New York: The Macmillan Company, 1943). Out of print.

WALTER H. MOBERLY, *The Crisis in the University* (New York: The Macmillan Company, 1949).

A. JOHN COLEMAN, *The Task of the Christian in the University* (New York: Association Press, 1947). Out of print.

GEORGE H. WILLIAMS, *The Theological Idea of the University,* The Commission on Higher Education, National Council of the Churches of Christ. Revised from an article in *The Harvard Divinity School* (Boston: Beacon Press, 1954), entitled "An Excursus: Church, Commonwealth and College: The Religious Sources of the Idea of the University."

Additional

H. RICHARD NIEBUHR, *Christ and Culture* (New York: Harper & Brothers, 1951).

PHILIP E. JACOB, *Changing Values in College:* an Exploratory Study of the Impact of College Teaching (New York: Harper & Brothers, 1958).

DAVID RIESMAN, *Constraint and Variety in American Education* (Lincoln, Nebr.: University of Nebraska Press, 1956) and (New York: Doubleday Anchor, 1958).

* * *

An Annotated Bibliography on *Religion in Education* was compiled by Joseph Politella and published by the American Association of Colleges for Teacher Education in 1956.

ENDPIECE

I know the ways of learning; both the head
And pipes that feed the press, and make it run;
What reason hath from nature borrowed,
Or of itself, like a good housewife, spun
In laws and policy; what the stars conspire,
What willing nature speaks, what forced by fire;
Both th'old discoveries and the new-found seas,
The stock and surplus, cause and history—
All these stand open, or I have the keys:
Yet I love Thee.

(*The Pearl. Matthew xiii.* George Herbert, *1593-1633*.)